The Non-Negotiable: Educating African-American Male Students K-12

DR. LAWRENCE V. BOLAR

authorHOUSE®

AuthorHouse™
1663 Liberty Drive
Bloomington, IN 47403
www.authorhouse.com
Phone: 1 (800) 839-8640

Published by AuthorHouse 01/21/2017

ISBN: 978-1-5246-5917-2 (sc)
ISBN: 978-1-5246-5916-5 (e)

Library of Congress Control Number: 2017900417

Print information available on the last page.

This book is printed on acid-free paper.

"I am not a product of my circumstances. I am a product of my decisions."

—Stephen Covey

TABLE OF CONTENTS

Parent Page of Honor

Ephesians 6:4
Fathers, do not provoke your children to anger, but bring them up in the discipline and instruction of the Lord.

Life as an African American male comes with many challenges visible and non-visible. All challenges can be met with the help of Christ Jesus and parents who care.

One simply cannot control who their parents are however; one can choose to become the parent they wanted or desired to have!

Deuteronomy 6:6–7
And these words that I command you today shall be on your heart. You shall teach them diligently to your children, and shall talk of them when you sit in your house, and when you walk by the way, and when you lie down, and when you rise.

Mr. and Mrs. Jerry and Debra Underwood

Mr. and Mrs. Ray and Karlyn Smith

Mr. and Mrs. Curtis & Betty Jackson

Mr. Johnny Myers & Mrs. Johnnie Mae Myers Bolar Smith

Psalms 127:3
Behold, children are a heritage from the LORD, The fruit of the womb a reward.

> Everybody can be great. Because anybody can serve. You don't have to have a college degree to serve. You don't have to make your subject and your verb agree to serve.... You don't have to know the second theory of thermodynamics in physics to serve. You only need a heart full of grace. A soul generated by love.
>
> **– Martin Luther King, Jr.**

ACKNOWLEDGEMENT / DEDICATION PAGE

THE NON- NEGOTIABLE of Educating African American male students K-12 is dedicated to all of the many shoulders from which it was created. The ability to produce a project of this capacity begin with inspiration and determination from Christ Jesus, my awesome family and loved ones. I share this project with educators like, Frederick Douglass, Booker T. Washington, W.E.B. Du Bois, Dr. Martin Luther King Jr., President Barak Obama, Ola Mae Robinson (My 5th grade teacher), Dr. Elaine Johnson, my spiritual educator, Dr. James Harris, my mentor, Christian Bolar, Caleb Boston, Caleb Carpenter, Jerion Underwood, Aaron M. Reid, Ja'Bril Scott and Damion Lewis. My prayer is that this book provides the internal and external manifestation that germinates inside of each reader that transforms the mind of each reader.

Thank you and may God Bless the reader and hearer of this message.

Job 36:12 English Standard Version (ESV)
12 But if they do not listen, they perish by the sword and die without knowledge.

> "Tell me and I forget; show me and I remember;
> involve me and I understand."
>
> **–Anonymous**

ABSTRACT

THE NO CHILD Left Behind Act (NCLB), instituted in 2002 by President George W. Bush, has caused a world wind of pros and cons, as well as education reform. Education today is considerably different from education ten to twenty years ago. NCLB has provided some alarming data concerning African American males' achievement gaps that can no longer be ignored.

This book on the Non-Negotiable of Educating African American males will highlight several salient points that were stimulated by NCLB. The United States Census Bureau projects that by 2050 about 50 percent of the U.S. population will be African American, Hispanic, or Asian. Along with this information, several alarming problems are presented. One problem is the dropout rate; research indicates that 53 percent of African American males nationwide drop out of school. African American high school students are falling significantly behind their Caucasian counterparts in graduation rates, literacy rates, and college preparedness rates, while leading them in dropout rates. In 2005, 55 percent of all black students graduated from high school on time with a regular diploma, compared to 78 percent of whites. In 2005, the on-time graduation rate for black males was 48 percent nationally; for white males it was 74 percent. According to the Schott 50 State Report on Public Education and Black Males, African American and Hispanic 12th grade students read at approximately the same level as Caucasian 8th grade students. The National Assessment of Educational Progress reports that 88 percent of African American 8th graders read below grade level, compared to 62 percent of Caucasian 8th graders.

The goal of this book is to afford each reader the opportunity to cultivate their educational outlook on African American males and provide their schools with effective cultural responsive reform.

> Before stop-and-frisk tactics were deemed unconstitutional in New York City by a Supreme Court judge in 2013, 54 percent of the 191,588 New Yorkers stopped-and-frisked by police that year were black while only 11 percent of searches involved white people.

A Snap Shot of the problems African American males face

According to the National Association for the Advancement of Colored People (NAACP), African Americans constitute nearly 1 million of the total 2.3 million incarcerated population, and have nearly six times the incarceration rate of whites.[4] A 2013 study confirmed that black men were much more likely to be arrested and incarcerated than white men, but also found that this disparity disappeared after accounting for self-reported violence and IQ.[5] An August 2013, Sentencing Project report on Racial Disparities in the United States Criminal Justice System, submitted to the United Nations, found that "one of every three black American males born today can expect to go to prison in his lifetime".[6][7]

- One out of nine African American men will be in prison between the ages of 20 and 34.[8]
- Black males ages 30 to 34 have the highest crime rate of any race/ethnicity gender and age combination. (According to America Community Survey.)
- "In 2014, 6% of all black males ages 30 to 39 were in prison, compared to 2% of Hispanic and 1% of white males in the same age group."[9]
- "The Lifetime chances of going to prison are 32.2% for Black males and 17.2% for Latino males, while only 5.9% for White males." (Finzen 301)
- 1 in 3 black males will go to prison in their lifetime. (Sentencing Project)
- Incarceration by race and ethnicity

2010. Inmates in adult facilities, by race and ethnicity. Jails, and state and federal prisons.[10]			
Race, ethnicity	% of US population	% of U.S. incarcerated population	National incarceration rate (per 100,000 of all ages)
White (non-Hispanic)	64	39	450 per 100,000
Hispanic	16	19	831 per 100,000
Black	13	40	2,306 per 100,000

"An investment in knowledge always pays the best interest."

–Benjamim Franklin

INTRODUCTION

The Non-Negotiables of Educating African American Male Students K-12 to include the Bolar Theory

THE OVERARCHING GOAL for this book is to bring enlightenment to a dark cloud that hovers over the success or lack of success of the African American male student. Do all African American male students become statistics of the school system-prison pipeline, their environments, societal norms, and the criminal justice system? The answer is a resounding no. However, far too many of them have and continue to do so for various reasons that this book will uncover and explore.

The Bolar Theory

The African American male is a very complicated and complex individual. The complications often begin long before birth but increase while in his mother's womb based on his extremely diverse and complex environment. The environmental factors multiply and become increasingly more intense based on the challenges of societal norms. The societal norms are often instilled in him upon arrival to the public school system; a system that is not properly prepared to educate a student who finds it challenging to receive lecture-based instruction, often described as the "sit and get."

The Bolar Theory is based upon foundational structures that either don't exist or exist on a very low level. Case in point, African American males are often born to unwed mothers. These unwed mothers, who are often underage, may not be cognitive or financially stable enough to clearly understand or provide the foundational infrastructure needed for African American male students to be successful. The infrastructure I speak of can be understood by the simple comparison of babysitting with a family member as opposed to being in a structured educational instructional institute, such as a pre-school. Some public schools do provide a free pre-school program, however, often there is a long waiting list to get into these programs. The students who cannot get into the free public school pre-school programs often stay home with a family member or friend. These young African American male boys often stay with a paid babysitter who may or may not offer any structured or educational instruction. African American boys being reared under these conditions often run around playing and watching TV all day.

Envision for a moment two energetic and healthy young boys starting kindergarten for the first time with the same teacher under the same conditions. Boy A has been staying home with an older lady who allows him to watch TV and play all day until his parent picks him up. Boy B has been going to a Christian preschool for the last year and a half. In his preschool he had to recite the Pledge of Allegiance, learn to write his name, spell words, do math problems, and recite his numbers and ABCs every day. Can we truly expect both boys to perform at the same level and if so, what does this look like?

The transition of a child who enters kindergarten for the very first time without any formal instruction looks totally different. One child has been introduced to educational structure with routines, expectations, and procedures. Picture for a moment the challenges Boy A must be facing. He has never been held accountable for having to sit down for longer than five to ten minutes at a time, not even when he eats his lunch. Boy A eats his lunch standing and walking around playing with random toys. The same boy has never worked on reading, writing, spelling his name, phonetic sounds, or attempted to read or be read to on a regular basis.

Boy B, on the other hand, has to sit down at the table and remain until all students have eaten. Boy B has to line up in a single file line and quietly walk back to class. Once he arrives to class he is asked to take out his storybook and listen to his teacher read and follow along. The teacher introduces and uses context clues to check for understanding, and helps with understanding what's being read. The teacher asks probing questions to ensure that the young boy understands what is being taught. Boy B now has to color a picture out of the book he read and explain why he chose what colors he used.

Boy A has been picked up from the babysitter and arrives home to do the same thing over again until bedtime. For example, Boy A continues to play and run through the house doing what he feels like doing and just simply having fun, jumping off the sofa or playing with toys before going to bed.

Boy B has been picked up from his pre-school program and returns home to a similar but different routine. Boy B plays most of the evening as well, however, he has to sit and read or be read to. Boy B has to watch educational shows on TV or on an iPad before going to bed.

In conclusion, when we compare the two boys we see the similarities and differences that impede or promote their educational success. One cannot begin to understand the disparities of African American male students without gaining a clear understanding of their foundations.

The Non-Negotiables begin with:

1. **Do not let what they look like or say intimidate you!**
2. **Create multiple opportunities to forge strong meaningful relationships!**
3. **Trust, mutual respect, and genuine care about their well-being and their future is imperative!**

"Education is an ornament in prosperity and a refuge in adversity."

–Aristotle

CHAPTER ONE

Historical Overview in African American Education from 1900's to 2017

GLOBAL SYSTEMIC SUSTAINED educational reform for the 21st century African American male student cannot be instituted unless everyone unequivocally understand from whence African Americans have come. The struggle and the dream of all African Americans still exist today in 2017.

In the early 1900s, debate flourished within the African-American community regarding education. In the 1900s, African-Americans were kept at their inferior status because (a) poll taxes prevented them from voting due to a lack of money, (b) literacy tests hindered their ability to vote because of an inability to read, and (c) residency requirements disqualified them to vote because of a lack of property (Thernstrom & Thernstrom, 1997). During the 1900's, African-Americans had little to no access to government provided education (Lomotey, 2010). African- Americans who wanted an education knew the importance of education and worked to build schools within their own communities (Lomotey, 2010). The schools could only offer African-Americans basic reading, writing, and mathematics. Most

African-Americans could not advance their skill levels to compete in business or professional interactions (Lomotey, 2010). The two advocates at the forefront of education were W.E.B. Du Bois and Booker T. Washington; "they sharply disagreed on strategies for African-Americans social and economic progress" (Two Nations of Black America).

Washington "preached a philosophy of self-help, racial solidarity and accommodation" which suggested African-Americans disregard racial inequality and focus on becoming a better person and monetary gain (Two Nations of Black America). Washington founded Tuskegee Institute and urged industrial education, "where self-help was preached as gospel and where students and faculty combined strenuous outdoor labor with their intellectual endeavors" (Brands, p. 422). President Theodore Roosevelt was so impressed with Washington's views and strong influence in the African-American community; he invited Washington to the White House to share his perspective for African-American advancement in 1901. Roosevelt would come to view this meeting as a political misstep and never offered another invitation to Washington or any other individual of color to the White House. President Roosevelt's action reveals the limited role African-Americans played in the American education system (Two Nations of Black America).

DuBois believed "Washington's strategy would serve only to perpetuate white oppression" and individual action was necessary (Two Nations of Black America). DuBois and others founded the National Association for the Advancement of Colored People (NAACP) because they believed in education and supported advancement in the arts and sciences. According to DuBois, "social change could be accomplished by developing the small group of college-educated blacks he called [the Talented Tenth]" (Two Nations of Black America. p. 3). Progress would be made only through excellence and hard work. The philosophies of Washington and DuBois separated people into the radical and conservative wings (Two Nations of Black America). This division in the African-American community weakened social and political advancement in public education for African-Americans (Two Nations of Black America).

Brown vs. Board of Education

Fifty-three years after Washington and DuBois' efforts to promote African-American education, education changed forever with the court ruling in 1954: *Brown vs. the Topeka Board of Education.* This ruling is the single most important court ruling in the history of American education (Alvarez & Brown, 2002; Blanchett, Brantlinger, & Shealey, 2005). In 1951, in Topeka, Kansas, thirteen parents in proxy for their twenty children started a lawsuit against the school board against segregated schools (Alvarez & Brown, 2002). The lawsuit demanded public policy to reverse racial segregation. Kenneth Clark's statement was a key component in the ruling. Clark, a psychologist, conducted a psychological test with dolls. The result of the test demonstrated how African-American students correlated good behavior with white dolls and bad behavior with black dolls (Clark & Clark, 1947). The decision by the Supreme Court was that segregation based on race was unconstitutional. According to Chief Justice Earl Warren, "To separate them from others of similar age and qualifications solely because of their race generates a feeling of inferiority as to their status in the community that may affect their hearts and minds in a way unlikely to ever be undone" (Clark & Clark, 1947).

Public Education in the 21st Century

According to Curry, the American public education still needs help sixty years after *Brown vs. Board of Education.* Curry indicated that the Brown case is still relevant and each new generation needs to be reminded that separate but equal is generally not equal. Each successive generation of educators should not simply celebrate the passage of *Brown vs. Board of Education*, but be aware of the complexity of the ruling and its impact on today's educational system. According to curry, Brown was necessary to correct the lack of many basic civil and equal rights for the African-American. However, in the process of providing this remedy, sufficient efforts were not provided nor were problems acknowledged regarding ancillary consequences of the court action. The appointment and equal opportunity of African-American principals and teachers still remain a continued need. As the nation's schools have entered the 21st century, student populations have become more diverse (Curry, 2004).

According to Hamlet (2012), article on Exploration of African-American males and the influence of race, gender and teacher beliefs about their academic success, there has not been a shortage of calls to improve teaching. Based on the federal law, the *No Child Left Behind Act* has mandated that school systems have highly qualified teaching in the nation's public schools. Although the question still remains, "What makes an effective teacher, particularly of African-American males in an urban environment?" Hamlet indicated that African-American males in public schools are the hardest hit, having the lowest achievement rates on standardized tests and the highest dropout rates of approximately 50% or more. Hamlet's research states, that the majority comes from low social economic status and single parent families, having limited learning resources and facilities at home. Hamlet indicated that their behavior leads to frequent suspensions, transfers, and eventually many of them drop out from school before graduating.

"Education is the most powerful weapon you can use to change the world."

–Nelson Mandela

CHAPTER TWO

Why is Educating African American Males an Important Topic?

THE UNITED STATES has struggled with its responsibility of educating African American students. How do we know the struggle exists? Because there is a national crisis in which academic difficulty and school failure is disproportionately high among African American males across the United States. In research done in an effort to improve the education of African American male students, increasing evidence suggests that multiple factors prevent the success of African American male students. One of these factors is a cultural aspect: students' learning styles. Educators who fail to recognize the impact learning styles have on achievement levels in classrooms promote continued failure amongst African American male students.

Another academic indicator to factor in is that students transitioning from middle school to high school face a range of academic and social challenges that impact learning styles and success. And this is the case for African American male students as well. The academic content is more diverse and challenging, and the instructional delivery is increasingly text-based, requiring competence in literacy and problem-solving skill areas. Students entering 9th grade often struggle to find an appropriate peer group and may face challenges in the community and at home, such as poverty, which hinders motivation and diminishes school engagement. The combined and interrelated challenges of poor achievement and low school engagement increase the likelihood of dropping out.

The Non-negotiable of educating African American males is such a critical topic facing our nation today. Why is this topic so critical? The topic is so critical because the African American male student is in serious trouble. In fact, they're no longer in trouble; they're in danger of being educationally wiped-out. Based on the majority of national research today, African American males continue to be disproportionately incarcerated, policed, and sentenced to death at significantly higher rates than their white counterparts. This is certainly not all about race but when making a casual comparative analysis one normally looks at the highs and the lows. The Caucasian male happens to be the highest and the African American male is the lowest. These comparisons will continue throughout the book and it has absolutely nothing to do with racism. However, in order to understand the Non-Negotiable of Educating African American males you must get a glimpse of what life looks like in their world. The media also causes negative perceptions. Think about how often you see positive images of African American males in the media. It is very rare. A sighting of Elvis Presley is more likely, a look-alike that is. One of the things I would strongly recommend is that teachers, school counselors, and administrators take a ride through some of the communities that African American males live in. Of course, we do have some African American males who live in areas where the social economic statures are high. However, riding through the inner-city neighborhoods and communities they're more often found in can be quite an eye opener. Some school districts make this mandatory for new teachers.

Please brace yourself for the journey down the African American male national statistical road; it's going to be bumpy. According to recent data by the Department of Education, African American students are arrested far more often than their white classmates. The data showed that 96,000 students were arrested and 242,000 referred to law enforcement by schools during the 2009-10 school year. Of those students, black and Hispanic students made up more than 70 percent of arrested or referred students. Harsh school punishments, from suspensions to arrests, have led to high numbers of youth of color coming into contact with the juvenile justice system and at an earlier age.

Note: Thoughts based on this statement.

____

____

____

____

____

____

____

____

____

According to the Bureau of Justice Statistics, one in three black men can expect to go to prison in their lifetime. Individuals of color have a disproportionate number of encounters with law enforcement, indicating that racial profiling continues to be a problem. A report by the Department of Justice found that blacks and Hispanics were approximately three times more likely to be searched during a traffic stop than white motorists. African Americans were twice as likely to be arrested, and almost four times as likely to experience the use of force during encounters with the police. The prison population grew by 700 percent from 1970 to 2005, a rate that is outpacing crime and population rates. The incarceration rates are one in every fifteen African American men and one in every thirty-six Hispanic men are incarcerated in comparison to one in every one hundred six white men.

Note: Thoughts based on this statement.

____

____

____

____

____

____

____

____

____

In light of these disparities, it is imperative that criminal justice reform via education evolves as the foremost civil rights issue of the 21st century. The reason this is of grave importance is because if it doesn't, African American males are doomed. The education of African American students was once thought of as the key to success for all African Americans but today we see a philosophy that is uniquely different and rightfully so. The data shows some of the various reasons why the African American philosophy has changed so drastically towards education. The overarching goal here is to cause a renewal of mind and love for education in the African American male student. There have been a number of initiatives on the state and federal levels to address the racial disparities in youth incarceration, but there is still so much more that can be done and that needs to be done to change the mindset of African American male students.

Note: Thoughts based on this statement.

____

____

____

____

____

____

____

____

____

Former Secretary of Education Arne Duncan announced the Schools Discipline Initiative to bring increased awareness of effective policies and practices to ultimately dismantle the school-to-prison pipeline. So what is the school-to-prison pipeline? The school-to-prison pipeline refers to policies and practices that push students, particularly the most vulnerable and at-risk, out of the classroom and into the juvenile and criminal justice system. So who are these students? According to the *Fact Sheet: How Bad is the School-to-Prison Pipeline?* "The school-to-prison pipeline: an epidemic that is plaguing schools across the nation. Far too often, students are suspended, expelled, or even arrested for minor offenses that leave visits to the principal's office a thing of the past. Statistics reflect that these policies disproportionately target students of color and those with a history of abuse, neglect, poverty, or learning disabilities."

States like California and Massachusetts are considering legislation to address the disproportionate suspensions among students of color. And in Clayton County, Georgia, collaborative local reforms have resulted in a 47 percent reduction in juvenile court referrals and a 51 percent decrease in juvenile felony rates. These initiatives could serve as models of success for lessening the disparities in incarceration rates.

Note: Thoughts based on this statement.

____

____

____

____

____

____

____

____

____

Good News

The high school dropout rate for African American males has actually hit a historic low. According to a 2013 *Education Week* study, about 62 percent of African Americans completed high school in 2010 (the most recent year for which the necessary data was available), compared to 80 percent of white students. The increase represents a 30 percent narrowing of the gap between black and white high school students. African American men are grossly overrepresented in the penal system; however, there are more African American males in college than in prison, as of 2011. Howard University professor Ivory A. Toldson found in his research that there are about 600,000 more African American males enrolled in higher education than are in jail.

Note: Thoughts based on this statement.

____

____

____

____

____

____

____

____

____

CHAPTER THREE

The Perception of the African American Male Student

PERCEPTION IS A problem most of us face today no matter where we come from or what our ethnicity is. However, when it comes to African American male students in public education, I believe perception is taken to a whole new level across our great nation. This perception is not reality, but it is often viewed in such a manner because of the disjointed relationship between the African American male students and the Caucasian educator. The African American male students have continued to struggle because of the nature of the relationship between the two, and although society has tried to hide it and deny that it exists, it does not negate the data that comes from the cultural barriers the group faces. I'm reminded of the popular commercial aired during the Christmas holiday season where Santa Claus and the M&M characters run into each other and they are so shocked to find that the other exists that they both pass out. This is similar to the reaction many Caucasian people have when told they are just as accountable for the lack of success of African American male students, I believe this is because of the deep-rooted cultural differences between the two groups.

In the real world, with the increased use of social media, we can now see African American males being abused, mistreated, and senselessly killed all over our great nation via Facebook, Instagram, Snapchat, and live video screenings on iPhones and other electronic devices. When young African American males like Trayvon Martin and so many others are killed with no true justification or vindication through our judicial system, it truly has a major effect on the mindsets of all parties. The African American males feel hopeless, afraid, and mistrustful of the Caucasian male and female who are in positions of authority and render the punishment for these crimes committed by other Caucasian Americans. The flip side is that Caucasian Americans are equally afraid of African American males because of the lack of compliance to their direction or directives. Both groups are really just afraid, and when people are afraid it's hard to connect or communicate effectively. The news and social media has created in the minds of most people, including Caucasian female educators, that all African American males are lazy, unmotivated, shiftless, prison-bound thugs and drug dealers, without taking the time to meet them where they are and guide them where they need be. These perceptions even exist in the lives of professional African American males who have to work ten times harder than their Caucasian counterparts. This has been seen with President Barrack Obama who had to endure things that no other president has had to deal with in order to get congressional support or approval.

The school-to-prison pipeline, where we often see young African American males serving long, harsh sentences for crimes far less heinous than those of their Caucasian counterparts, is another product of this fear. This is not perception—it's reality—as we continue to fight through the alarming data about African American males in public education.

For a professional educator there should be a greater level of urgency in the opportunity and responsibility to secure a positive functioning relationship. The perception of some Caucasian female educators is that African American males all want to fail and are solely responsible for their failure or lack of educational success. I certainly believe the blame has to be shared with the Caucasian female. The working professional educator recognizes the problem firsthand but often fails to believe they can make a difference. The Caucasian female aids in the African American male's lack of success based on her inability as a trained professional to create opportunities to build strong relationships with African American males and help them succeed.

Note: Thoughts based on this statement.

____

____

____

____

____

____

____

____

____

Inspiration Behind the Creation: The Non-Negotiable of Educating African American Males

The Non-Negotiable of Educating African American Males is a project I have worked on my entire career. My twenty-two years of education has consisted of working with some of the most challenging African American males and minority students in the schools and community I served. Thus far, several of the school districts I have been afforded the opportunity to work in have bolstered a heavy African American population with an increase in Hispanic population. This disclaimer shares that I have had a wealth of experience in working with the topic and population. I will be the first to admit that I don't know everything, and that my experience and the populations I have been exposed to are extremely small in comparison to national data. When examining the national data I can safely say the problems exist in both rural, urban, and suburban populations.

One could easily assume that their school and/or school district do not have these challenges because of their limited African American male population. However, that is simply not the case! The problem exists everywhere but because your African American male student population and/or your Hispanic male population percentages are average to low, it does not get as much attention. Oh, but the problem is there. The problem can be camouflaged in schools and districts that have high social economic statues as well. The schools that garner most, if not all, the negative attention are schools that are in districts with heavy poverty. Therefore, reform has to be for all schools, not just the ones with alarming numbers.

Let me be the first to profess and confess unequivocally that African American male students can be extremely challenging for anyone to work with for a number of reasons. On the other hand some of them are the most creative, talented, and critical thinking students I have ever worked with. I love the teaching and learning process and I love all students, however, African American Males can be a handful at times to relate to or work with, even for me, an experienced African American male educator. The real challenges come into play when people stereotype all of them as being lazy, thugs, gang members, criminals who lack motivation, or assume they all listen to gangster rap music, sag their pants, and simply don't care. A lot of these are just plain old misconceptions, false perceptions, and myths—not reality. Often, images in the media only show African American males in negative images and interactions, where they oppose authority, sell and do drugs, or commit violent crimes. This is why misconceptions are often taken for reality by some people. In order to understand the non-negotiables of educating African American male students, or any student for that matter, we must take the time to get to know them. This can be done by seeking first to understand who they are, where they have been, and where they need to be. Most of all, don't be afraid of what they look like, sound like, or smell like. The reality is, there are some very critical cultural disconnections that illuminate when a lack of relationship exists.

> "Self-confidence is the most attractive quality a person can have. How can anyone see how awesome you are if you can't see it yourself?"
>
> **–Unknown**

When conversations about African American males are brought up, typically there's a negative connotation instantly attached to this group, and rightfully so for a number of reasons. This did not just start happening overnight; it's been this way for quite some time. In fact, I contemplated naming this book The Non-Negotiable of Educating Minority Males, however, I decided not to use this title for a number of reasons. The rationale behind my contemplation of using this alternative name was to be politically correct. The problem is that we have been politically correct for too long. The reality is that African American male students have the greatest need and there is no reason to cover it. I often get the impression that people like using the term *minority* when they want to cover the problem our country is having, or when they want to soft sell this alarming problem.

The elephant in the room that everyone wants to avoid is very scary. I have been in division level meetings where it becomes incredibly tense to even talk about the needs of African American males. This has been my experience working as an executive level intern for a full academic school year in a division that bolsters a heavy Caucasian population of students along with a majority Caucasian executive level team. When having conversation about this topic everyone appeared to become very sensitive as if Pandora's Box had been opened.

Note: Thoughts based on this statement.

> "When a black voice is raised in protest to oppression, those who are comfortable with our oppression are the first to criticize us for daring to speak out against it."
>
> **–Harry Belafonte**

CHAPTER FOUR

A Didactic Look at Who Educates African American Male Students

UNDERSTANDING THE DISPARITIES of African American males is a very important body of research. I'm confident that this research is something every educator should be exposed to. My only request is as you read this book, read with an open mind and don't allow racism or biases to blur your thinking. Recognize the true value of this book and what it was constructed to do.

When we look at African American males educationally they are failing nationally in every category. Educational scholars are everywhere and no one really seems to be able to come up with a valid solution for resolving this enormous problem. Nationally the public school system as a whole keeps coming up short as it relates to African American male students and, quite frankly, as an African American male educator it is disheartening not to be able to see or envision the end of this alarming epidemic. I sincerely believe that these gaps can be closed given the proper attention needed within our educational institutions. These gaps can be decreased significantly with just a few minor adjustments.

This body of work is near and dear to my heart for a number of reasons. The number one reason is because I am an educator who has been in the teaching and learning business for over two decades and I simply love learning and I love teaching. As a reflective practitioner, I have had the unique opportunity to read, research, and study the work of some of the most prolific educational scholars of the 21st century, including Marzano, Strong, and Harris. Over the last twenty-one years I have adopted, borrowed, and utilized their strategies to aid me as an instructional leader. The second reason this body of literature is important to me is because I am an African American male who seeks to motivate, support, guide, and direct educators who have challenges working with African American males.

So where do we begin with addressing this problem of educating African American male students? Professionally I believe we have to begin with those who teach African American male students and the impact these educators have on the student's growth or lack thereof. According to the National Center for Education Statistics, in the 2007-2008 school year the total number of teachers in the United States was 3,898,420. This number is broken down by percentage according to race:

White, non-Hispanic – 83.5 percent

Black, non-Hispanic – 6.7 percent

Native American or Alaskan Native, non-Hispanic – 0.5 percent

Asian, non-Hispanic – 1.3 percent

Native Hawaiian or other Pacific Islander, non-Hispanic – 0.2 percent

Hispanic, regardless of race – 6.9 percent

Two or more races, non-Hispanic – 0.9 percent

Research indicates the teaching and learning business is led and directed primarily by Caucasian females. Comprising 83.5 percent of all teachers, Caucasians dominate the educational profession by a very large margin. No other group comes remotely close to this number. The next question then has to be, where is the disconnection with the Caucasian female teachers and the African American male students and how can this question be strategically be addressed?

What exactly does this mean? It means there is a disconnect between the Caucasian female teacher and the African America male student. Of course it does not take a rocket scientist to recognize the disconnect begins here. No matter who thinks or believes otherwise, the proof is in the data. Educators have to create opportunity along with professional development to close the disconnection between themselves and their African American male students; 83.5 percent of the teaching and learning profession (give or take a few percentages based on the year of the data you're examining) must shoulder some responsibility for the failure of the African American male student. This is not meant to be a fault-finding query but if the gap ever has any chance of closing this is the first place to begin.

The most current national data statistics state that 84 percent of classroom teachers are Caucasian females while less than two percent are African American males. One must ask the question, where does the responsibility for the lack of success lie and with whom? Because African American males are failing in all categories, one could easy assume or assess that Caucasian females cannot or have not been able to teach African American males. Of course no one wants to mention this or even consider this as the reason behind the lack of success African American males in our country have been facing. I do believe a huge part of the solution begins with providing intense relationship building training for Caucasian female teachers, counselors, and administrators, specifically geared toward the academic and social success of African American male students. The training should be encouraged and secured in school districts across our nation. I'm confident if the training is properly unpacked, received, and enforced the gaps would begin to close immediately. Remember, students really don't care how much you know; they want to know how much you care. I sincerely believe this is one of the top three reasons the disconnect exists. Until educators across this great nation of ours acknowledge this as a part of the problem no change can take place. In my research and experience, I've found that the missing link is the relationship. The lack of relationship often promotes a lack of respect for authority. Students who don't respect you have a very difficult time listening to you or following your directions. In fact, because of certain very unique cultural differences, African American males respond totally different to directives from Caucasian teachers and administrators. This usually results in African American male students being misunderstood, over-diagnosed in special education, and suspended from schools more often than any of their counterparts. One very unique cultural difference is that oftentimes African American mothers give out directives that are non-negotiable, so to speak. Caucasian teachers give out options. From the onset this doesn't sound like a huge problem, but it is. Giving a directive says: *This is the expectation. You don't have to like it; you just have to meet it.* There is no room for negotiation. Simply put, it means get it done. The Caucasian female offers options and allows wiggle room for not meeting the expectations to excel or succeed. Is this a bad practice? No, not for all students, but it certainly is for most African American male students. Why? Because in most cases, their entire lives have revolved around the relationship with their African American mothers, who don't have time or energy to negotiate with them.

Former Secretary of State Arne Duncan led the charge on recruiting more African American males into the education profession as a solution to the problem.

Could he have simply stated that the Caucasian female has been a direct cause for African American male students' failure? Yes, he could have and yes, I believe he should have! Would that have resolved the problem? No, it would not have. However, I'm confident that it would have brought some much-needed attention to the issue.

One of the most important factors in the non-negotiable of educating African American males is not to point fingers or play the blame game. There are many broken pieces needed to repair the problem our country is facing when it comes to the success of African American males. The key component this body of literature hopes to expose is centered on building strong positive relationships. Repairing the disconnection problem between the Caucasian female and the African American male could yield a significant increase in the success of the African American male student. A missing link, hindering the success of the African American male student, is the need to improve the relationship between the African American male student and his Caucasian female teacher.

How do we begin to repair this problem? First, by recognizing there is a problem. However, the question has to be posed: does the Caucasian female teacher have the capacity to successfully teach the African American male student? The answer is a resounding yes. One of the leading beliefs propelling this research is in the need to increase the success rate for the African American male student. I strongly believe success lies within a collaborative approach. One important part of their success lies within the increase of African American male educators.

One could believe African American males are more likely to win the lottery than they are to have an African American male teacher. Most students aren't exposed to African American male teachers unless he is a P.E. teacher or a coach. Most of my research has been conducted with the goal of encouraging African American males to enter the education profession, to inspire them to be the parents that they wanted, and to be cognizant of the social perceptions and stigmas attached to their attire and demeanors. I have written and published several books centered on supporting African American males, such as *Eradicating the Saggy Pants Syndrome in America, No Parent Left Behind: Strategies of Success for the 21st Century Parent, and Nothing Substitutes Time*.

The third reason is that I was an African American male student who was educated in a system for twelve years where I managed to be exposed to only one African American male teacher, who just happened to be my ninth grade P.E. teacher and my football coach. I was taught in classrooms of twenty-five to thirty students, and these classrooms would consist of two African American males at the most.

The reason I chose to share this information is because of what I observed during my twelve-year tenure as a student. I was an ideal student athlete who very rarely had negative exchanges with students or staff, however this wasn't always the case with some of my African American male peers. Here is what I observed; I notice that there was this special bond that my Caucasian counterparts shared with our teachers. This bond or relationship appeared to be secretive and extremely special. The relationship would be similar to that of an uncle, aunt, or very close relative.

I could never understand why this relationship existed. No matter how closely I observed their interactions I could not figure it out or put my finger on the reasoning behind its existence. No matter how great of a student or athlete I was, it appeared impossible to obtain this relationship with my teachers. Let me be very clear; I had some awesome teachers and we shared mutual respect, understanding, and positive relationships. I'm certain other African American students experienced this, but just could not wrap their minds around what exactly was happening.

I did not understand in totality what was happening, and I did not discover what was happening until I was doing research for my dissertation. My dissertation topic was Motivating African American Males to Enter the K-5 Teaching Profession. For years, from high school to college, I observed this secret bond. One experience I remember in particular occurred when I was taking classes at the University of Southern Mississippi. The class had similar dynamics as my high school. The class at best consisted of two African American males. One day after class had been dismissed I lagged behind to have a conversation with the professor. Like so many times before, many of the Caucasian students stayed behind to chat with the professor as well. Of course there is nothing wrong with this and it's a great practice for all students, regardless of their race or nationality. However, what I noticed was here again was this unique relationship that my Caucasian counterparts had and that I longed for, and I could not understand why I couldn't obtain it.

"Education is our passport to the future, for tomorrow belongs to the people who prepare for it today."

–Malcom X

Note: Thoughts based on this statement.

CHAPTER FIVE

Understanding the Concept of the Similar-To-Me Effect and its Consequences

MY GOAL HERE is to introduce you to some very important research that I have uncovered. This research made a lot of since to me as an educator of twenty-plus years. I felt like I finally figured out what was going on and why I couldn't seem to grasp or obtain the same level of relationship my Caucasian counterparts shared with our teachers and professors. My experience attending a Historically Black College and University also validated this research. I will offer feedback on this statement at the end of the chapter after you have read a snapshot of the Similar-To- Me Effect (Williams 2012, Bolar 2015). Although some of the research in this study may be a bit dated, it is very impactful. The research by no means indicates that one race or ethnic group is superior in educating. The research is to aid in the effort to understand how to educate African American males. The other disclaimer is that in education reform repeats itself with different jargon, different people, and larger studies.

According to Williams' phenomenological study, African American male teachers are believed to be better prepared to increase the academic performance of African American male students than teachers of other ethnic groups and gender due to the similar-to-me effect. According to the similar-to-me effect, individuals have a tendency to respond more favorably to people who are similar to them (Williams, 2012). The similar-to-me effect is applicable in education because in the classroom the teacher is more likely to help students similar to them because they can build connections with little to no resistance. The relationship is commonly constructed on shared backgrounds and culture. According to Wentzel, students accept instruction, discipline, and criticism easier from people who look like them because they believe they have familiar backgrounds (Wentzel, 1999).

"Education is what remains after one has forgotten what one has learned in school."

—Albert Einstein

Note: Thoughts based on this statement.

As indicated by Wentzel, the similar-to-me effect is very much present and viable in teacher-student relationships from preschool through high school (Wentzel, 1999). The similar-to-me effect encourages positive teacher-student relationships that benefits the students academically and socially (Ladd et al, 1999). According to Hamre & Pianta, teachers and students having relationships built on the similar-to-me effect establish high levels of support and low levels of conflict. The high levels of support and the low levels of conflict lead to students attaining higher scores on measures of academics and behavioral adjustment than do students whose relationships with teachers are less positive (Hamre & Pianta, 2006).

"So often you find that the students you are trying to inspire, are the ones who end up inspiring you."

—Sean Junkins

Note: Thoughts based on this statement.

____

____

____

____

____

____

____

____

____

Quantitative research studies on teacher-student relationships provide statistics on the correlation between the lack of African American teachers at a school and the poor academic performance of African American male students at the same school (Corbett & Wilson, 2002). Corbett and Wilson also concluded that when African American male students associate and foster a relationship with African American male teachers, they increase in their academic performance and determination to be successful in school and the community. Hamre and Pianta (2006) discovered that a positive teacher-student relationship with the same race and gender could influence the students' opportunity for academic achievement up to eight years after the relationship. Ascher (1991) concluded when there is a limited presence of African American male teachers, the African American male students are more likely to be disinterested in school and more likely to be absent, which leads to decreased academic performance.

The K-12 teaching profession is dominated by white women, many who are very qualified and very interested in helping all their students succeed but lack the first-hand experience needed to connect with their Black male students.

Schools with majority African American male students also tend to have lower amounts of teachers who are certified in their degree areas. A U.S. Department of Education report found that in schools with at least 50 percent Black students, only 48 percent were certified in the subject, compared with 65 percent in majority white schools. In English, the numbers were 59 and 68 percent, respectively and in science, they were 57 percent and 73 percent.

"The purpose of education is to replace an empty mind with an open one."

–Malcolm Forbes

Note: Thoughts based on this statement.

Fremon & Hamilton noted that Caucasian teachers do not encourage or motivate African American students; however, African American male teachers do. Fremon and Hamilton (1997) insinuated that Caucasian teachers do not set high goals for African American male students; hence, the students are aware that the teacher has very low expectations and students have a tendency to work up to expectations resulting in low academic performance. Milner (2006) stated that teachers have the capability of giving students a sneak peak of what the future teacher will look like, good or bad. This example gives students an indication of what to look for in the future from their teachers. The expectation is to inspire students, however, according to Karunanayake & Nauta (2004) a role model will be inspirational only to the degree a person is able to identify similarities with the role model. Milner (2006) indicated that African American teachers are essential for the success of the African American student's academic achievement. They have the capacity to stimulate students to the degree that students remember and later refer back to the subject matter. One could conclude that Caucasian students succeed and surpass African American male students largely due to the similar-to-me effect. (Karunanayake & Nauta, 2004).

"When educating the minds of our youth, we must not forget to educate their hearts."

–Dalai Lama

Note: Thoughts based on this statement.

____

____

____

____

____

____

____

____

____

In classrooms that don't have African American teachers there is very little motivation for minority students to strive to be successful in the classroom (Martinez, 1991). In a school setting it's critically important for African American students to be able to relate to staff and administration to have a positive vision to emulate (Henze et al., 2002, p. 86). Often school-aged children, especially African American males, have a poor perception of school. This makes it extremely challenging for students to analyze educational concerns. Henze indicated that if the janitorial and cafeteria staff were all black individuals, nonwhite students would correlate their identity to that of submission without understanding the situation and may go on to believe they are not fit for other developed societal roles (Henze et al., 2002, p. 86).

> Let us look at education as a means to develop our greatest abilities, because in each of us there is a private hope and dream which, fulfilled, can be translated into benefit for everyone and greater strength for our entire nation.
>
> **–John F. Kennedy,**
> 35th President of the United States

Note: Thoughts based on this statement.

In order for a teacher to achieve and maintain positive outcomes in the classroom, teachers must hold and practice certain assumptions (Milner, 2006). Milner emphasized numerous ideas that led to the success of African American teachers with African American students. According to Milner, several considerations that teachers have include: (a) how to acquire and retain attention, (b) how to use shared culture to build a rapport, (c) how to set examples for successful development, (d) how to connect with parental figures, (e) how to hold students accountable, and (f) how to support their students.

Note: Thoughts based on this statement.

According to Nweke, Afolabi, Stewart, Stephens, & Toth (2004), to attract more African American males to the teaching field, recruitment efforts must be increased. There are several efforts in place to battle the scarcity of African American males in the classroom, including programs such as Troops-to-Teacher, Call Me Mister, and MenTeach. In addition, several networks and scholarships are being made available to help usher in a new generation of African American male teachers.

CHAPTER SIX

Strategies on How to Successfully Educate African American Male Students

EACH READER HAS had an opportunity to assess the historical disparities the African American male student has faced daily for years and continues to face today. This book has merely touched on the problem and why it exists, but there is so much more that has not been shared. The information presented prior to the strategies is extremely important and essential to know. One cannot begin to help with this emergent matter without having the opportunity to see how alarming the data really is. The unfortunate thing about this set of circumstances is that you have only gotten a snapshot of the African American male student's dilemma.

How do we begin to educate the African American male student? I believe this quote says it all: "Tell me and I forget; show me and I remember; involve me and I understand." – (Anonymous). This simple but powerful statement should be practiced by all educators. Students learn by social modeling and having their teachers check for understanding. Educators have to understand how to do simple show and tell and then check for their students' understanding of what was taught. Checking for understanding is critical but often forgotten after the showing and telling.

In three double-blind randomized field experiments, researchers at the University of Texas found that African American students improved their grades after having the assignment expectation reinforced by their teachers. These results point out that a cycle of mistrust and lower expectations is a likely culprit in cases of African American underperformance. The low expectations are often picked up quickly by students. I strongly believe that if you put high expectations in place then the students will meet them. No expectations lead to little or no result.

IN ORDER TO UNDERSTAND HOW TO EDUCATE AFRICAN AMERICAN MALES WE BEGIN WITH CONVERSATIONS WITH NONE OTHER THAN AFRICAN AMERICAN MALES

CHRISTIAN BOLAR, 4TH GRADE STUDENT AT CASHELL DONAHOE ELEMENTARY SCHOOL HENRICO, VIRGINIA

My name is Christian Bolar. I am a 4th grade scholar roll student at Cashell Donahoe Elementary School. I excel in public speaking, sports, and music as well. I love playing the keyboard, drums, and guitar. I became so passionate about music and sports that my parents decided to let me have private lessons. I can play most music by ear and find it really easy to do so. I'm always on the go, either going to church, music lessons, choir rehearsals, or football or basketball practice.

I know school is important because both of my parents work in the school system and they tell me this all the time. Sometimes I like school and sometimes I don't. I really like going to my special classes like PE, art, and music. I like these classes because we get to do really fun and creative things. The regular classroom setting is very different because we have to do a lot of sitting down, do worksheets, and listen to the teacher talk for long periods of time. I don't like having to sit down in class for long periods of time without getting up, moving around, or talking to my friends. I wish the teacher allowed us to move around and talk without fussing at us.

I really like math and science. I normally make all A's on my report card but sometimes I need improvement on my behavior. I don't really know why I can't seem to get an S in conduct. I try really hard to be good in class so my mom and dad will be proud of me but sometimes I get so excited to finally get to talk to my friends in class that the teacher has to speak to me. I usually end up getting in trouble for talking too much or playing. Sometimes, because I remember things, I try to tell the teacher but she doesn't like when I do that.

School can be fun but all we do is sit and listen to the teacher talk all the time. So, I figured if I rush and get my work done I can do something I want to do and not have to sit in my seat. Sometimes, I get in such a big hurry to finish my work that I forget to put my name on my paper. When I do this it's because I just want to be finished with my work but it causes me to make careless mistakes. I really just want to finish my work so I can do something else. Maybe if the teacher made teaching fun and exciting I would not rush through my work. It is not fun to just sit and listen to the teacher for so long. I like learning better by doing and not by just looking and listening.

JERION UNDERWOOD, 8TH GRADE STUDENT AT PICAYUNE JUNIOR HIGH SCHOOL PICAYUNE, MISSISSIPPI

My name is Jerion Underwood. I am in the 8th grade. I am currently a student at Picayune Junior High. Some students learn better in small classes. Students in smaller classes will have more help from the teacher. Some students don't learn in bigger classes because they are not getting as much help as they need. Students that don't understand would have no one-on-one with the teachers. If they would have more one-on-one time they would understand the topic better. Their grades would improve more. If the school provided more time in class they could learn at a better pace about that subject they're learning so they could study longer on that topic to get better in it. Teachers should stick to one subject longer before moving to the next thing and changing subjects so students can understand what they are learning.

DAMION LEWIS, 10TH GRADE STUDENT AT PICAYUNE MEMORIAL HIGH SCHOOL PICAYUNE, MISSISSIPPI

My name is Damion Lewis. I am a 15-year-old African American. I am from Gulfport, Mississippi but I currently live in Picayune, Mississippi. I attend Picayune Memorial High School. I am in the tenth grade. My grades are good but the question for everyone is what is the best way for students to learn? Some may say they work better with no help. Others may work better with help from a teacher or another peer. Well, I, personally, work better with help so I know for sure that my answer is right at all times. Teachers go to school board conferences to see what's the best way to teach, but the outcome may be different from what they intended. This is a quote from our former president, George Bush: "When it comes to the education of our children, failure is not an option. Basically, what he is saying is failure can't be an option if teachers are doing their job, and it is not always the teachers' fault. Some students just don't want to learn. In conclusion, the way students learn will not be able to be solved because everyone is different. With that being said, it's the teacher's job to try to help students in any type of way possible.

CALEB BOSTON, 10TH GRADE STUDENT AT PICAYUNE MEMORIAL HIGH SCHOOL PICAYUNE, MISSISSIPPI

My name is Caleb S. Boston and I am currently a sophomore at Picayune Memorial High School, in Picayune, MS. My career aspirations and interests lie in science and math, and while I am not sure what I will major in, my interest lies with biological science and/or engineering.

My personal interests include playing high school football, reading, and drawing. Currently, I am a member of The National Academy of Future Scientists and Technologists, The Society of Torch and Laurel, and the Beta Club. I also served on the Student Council for two years and am the recipient of the Duke Tip Award. I have excelled academically by maintaining an "A" average throughout school and have received numerous academic excellence awards.

Being a young, smart African-American male may be an abnormality to many people because they do not see "us". With being labeled black comes a plethora of stereotypes (i.e. thug, drug dealer, future inmate, gang member, and a danger to public safety) and smart is not one of them. My mother always told me that there were people who would always be jealous and try to stop me. Therefore, I stay focused on the big picture of finishing high school in the top of my class and going to a university after high school graduation.

My experience in school is normal. I go to school, get good grades, and have no disciplinary problems; pretty normal. My teachers, who have been mostly Caucasian females have always complimented me on my intellect. Me being smart and black is seen as a strange thing to the white and black community and is sometimes seen as an unprecedented event. However, my expectations of myself have always been high. There is one thing that I've noticed throughout my schooling. There is a shortage of African-American males in the advanced and AP classes such as honors English, honors algebra, AP government, or anatomy and physiology just to name a few. Oftentimes I have been the only black male in the classes surrounded by a few black females. One experience I normally have is that the Caucasian or Asian male students seem to not mind me being smart, but the African-American males seem to be intimidated by my intelligence and seem to think I am better than they are because of my mental prowess. For more African-American males to break the stereotypes, they and their parents need to be more involved in their academics. I find that the majority of African-American students dwell on sports, but without the brains the brawn cannot get the job done.

The students on the football team always mock me because I am smart. They say things such as "ask Caleb…he gets all the awards and is smart" or when I say a word that is unfamiliar to them they will say "here he goes again using those big words." I always try to give them encouragement in that they too can be smart if they apply themselves more academically. I like the fact that I defy many stereotypes that plague the African-American community in America. That is why I try to help as many of my people as I can so that America and the world can have a better image when they picture people of African-American descent, in particular males. I must admit that for years I struggled with my own insecurities feeling as if I was different, weird, strange, and that nobody really got me, but now I count my intelligence as a true blessing and am very grateful that God chose me.

AARON REID, 11TH GRADE STUDENT AT LC BIRD HIGH SCHOOL CHESTERFIELD, VA

My name is Aaron Reid, and I am a 16-year-old junior at LC Bird High School. I am what you call a well-rounded student. I am very involved in school and community activities and organizations. Throughout my academic career I have always been an honor student. I currently hold a 3.9 GPA. I recently have been inducted into several honor societies, including the National Honor Society, the German Honor society, and the National Society of High School Scholars.

I am a student athlete. I am a member of the varsity boys' volleyball team, and last year, the junior varsity baseball team. I am a member of the leadership council for the marching band and the tuba section leader. I am currently 3rd chair in the All-County band and 4th chair in the All-District band. I will be auditioning for the Summer Residential Governor's School for the Visual and Performing Arts. My goal is to be a member of the All-State Band this year.

I consider myself a visual and hands-on learner. Because of that, my science classes, band, and business/marketing classes have been very exciting for me this year. I enjoy working in groups and getting the opportunity to share what I have learned in presentation form. Educators should try to reach all of their students' learning styles and present their curriculum in a variety of ways.

I recently completed a project for my business/marketing class. I had to find ways to represent a baseball player. I have played the game of baseball since age six, and know the game well. I was able to draft a contract for my client and show ways that I planned to increase his popularity in the media.

When I am allowed to write or speak about topics that interest me, I am always successful.

I am currently researching colleges and universities to attend. I will major in communications and music. Howard University, Emerson College, and Berkley College of Music are on my college tour list.

CALEB CARPENTER, 11TH GRADE STUDENT AT MATOACA HIGH SCHOOL CHESTERFIELD, VA

Hello. My name is Caleb Carpenter. I am currently a student at Matoaca High School. I am a junior and plan to attend college once I graduate.

I am currently taking four advanced/honors classes, which include colonial U.S. history, economics and personal finance, marketing, and English. There are many factors and challenges that can affect kids being successful in honors classes. One of the challenges is the class/work load. In these college credit or honor classes, often the work required of the students is vigorous and challenging. It requires students to be really focused. Some people would say that being a minority would also negatively affect a student's success in honors classes. Many judge and say that being African American makes it more difficult to be successful in honors classes because of the material that is taught. For me, I believe being an African American in honors classes is an advantage. I say this because I can bring a new point of view to discussions, not just to subjects dealing with African American culture, but to other topics as well.

In my classes, my teachers can appease all different types of learning styles. I believe my teachers are effective. I am a hands-on learner who really enjoys interacting, talking, and doing the things we learn about. Not all teachers can teach for my learning type. Sometimes teachers are driven by school requirements, limited time, or they just don't know how to teach to engage students like me. My current teachers have found a way to pique my interest and make me want to continue to expand my knowledge.

Being a leader in my school is easy for me. My manner of speech, my personality, and being easily entrusted has caused me to be a leader. I am told that I am easy to talk to, which has gained the trust of many people from many walks of life. When I am in a conversation with people I share different perspectives with them about God and just simple things about life. With this influence I have with my peers I can give them direction. This can be a good and bad thing! It is my decision, and my plan is to use this gift to motivate people to do good.

There are many challenges to being a Christian in my school. These challenges include sex, drugs, money, friends, parties, and many more. This is all a test to throw you off track so that you will not be successful or survive life. In order for you to be protected from these pressures you must pray, read your word, and have a true relationship with God. Doing all these things it will not eliminate the pressures, but it will diminish the urge or the feeling of pressure to participate or agree.

I believe education is necessary. No matter your race, religion, or where you are from education should be a priority. My parents always tell me education is the key to life. I believe all young men who are aspiring to be something great but it appears they cannot be successful or people are telling them they can't do something—they can. All they must do is work hard in everything they do and I am sure they will succeed.

JA'BRIL SCOTT 10TH GRADE STUDENT AT FRANKLIN MILITARY ACADEMY RICHMOND, VA

My name is Ja'Bril Scott. I am 16 years old and currently a sophomore student at Franklin Military Academy. I have been blessed in so many ways I was named Top 7th grader of the year, 8th grade class president, also I have been included in the "United States Achievement Academy" book for 2012-2013 and 2013-2014. In addition I had the opportunity to sing the National Anthem for the Small Business Awards Banquet in 2014. I continue to strive for honor and scholar roll each year. During the summer of 2016 I participated and completed the Officers

Training Corps in Fort A.P. Hill Va. I am apart of the Tri-M music honor society, Franklin Military Academy choir, Franklin Military FM Stereo acapella group, Saber Team, Honor Guard, Drill Team, hold as the battalion S2 assistant for Franklin Military Academy, I am a member of the Richmond Boys Choir. I am currently enrolled in advanced/honors classes such as AP English, AP Chemistry, Honors Geometry, Economics and Personal Finance. Upon graduation I plan to serve in the Military and further my education in music and criminal justice to become a judge. There are many types of learning styles. I am a Social Learner. I believe I am a social learner because I love to interact with different people to get a job done. In life I feel you have to be able to communicate with different people and to interact with people, that's why I enjoy my teachers method of teaching with giving us the opportunity to work with each other as a group to accomplish the goal. Every since I started school my mother always told me to Learn, Pay attention, and to definitely be focused. Now I fully understand in order to learn what your instructor is teaching you, you have to pay attention, if you don't pay attention then you will never understand the work that is provided to you and you must always remain focus in order to move forward to the next level. Being a young black male you have to push hard to reach your goals. My goal is to continue to be an educated, well mannered, hardworking, with goals an being a leader to show others the right path to take. Lastly my favorite quote by Vince Lombardi "The price of success is hard work, dedication to the job at hand, and the determination that whether we win or lose. We have applied the best of ourselves to the task at hand."

UNDERSTANDING KINESTHETICS

Kinesthetic learners are learners who need body movement and hands-on work. This is also true for tactile learners and children who have been labeled dyslexic, ADD, and ADHD.

STRATEGIES: HELPING KINESTHETIC LEARNERS FOCUS IN THE CLASSROOM

1. Kinesthetic learners need to move. They wiggle, tap, swing their legs, bounce, and often just can't seem to sit still. They learn through their bodies and their sense of touch.
2. They have excellent "physical" memory–they learn quickly and permanently the things they DO as they are learning.
3. Kinesthetic Leaners are often gifted in athletics, dancing, and other physical activities.
4. They are generally very coordinated and have an excellent sense of their body in space and of body timing. They have great hand-eye coordination and quick reactions.
5. Teach them to use deep breathing and purposeful relaxation to help with focus.
6. Information they learned via body movement is stored in the brain and if the child repeats that movement, it will not only help them focus, but will also help them remember what they learned.
7. Use skits for learning concepts and gestures for learning sight words, for example. Body movement as they learn will hold their focus on the lesson.

8. They will focus more easily if they have objects to manipulate instead of always using pencil and paper.
9. Let them move! If you tell them they can stand up, swing their legs, or even pace the floor as long as they are not disrupting the other students, their performance will improve.
10. Use novelty and change when you teach lessons in order to help break up long periods of time when the students would be sitting in their desks.
11. Teach kinesthetic learners to visualize themselves doing what they are learning. If you are teaching them steps for solving a problem, have them go inside their imaginations and "see" themselves following the steps.
12. Their attention follows their hands. Teach them draw sketches or diagrams of what they are hearing in a lesson. Or, when doing a sheet of math problems, teach them to point to each problem they come to. Let them use flashcards with information they are learning. Teachers will be successful in reaching all their learners **at one time** if they will develop a teaching style that is a synthesis of methods that target the whole brain (Vark, 2016).

KINESTHETIC AND TACTILE LEARNERS LEARN BEST
WHEN USING BODY MOTIONS
AND VISUALS TO HOLD THEIR ATTENTION

TACTILE LEARNERS

1. Tactile learners are closely related to kinesthetic learners. The tactile style is more moderate involving fine motor movements rather than whole body movement.
2. They learn primarily through the sense of touch.
3. They learn best through hands-on activities.
4. They express their learning best with projects they make, such as mini-books, games, dioramas, skits, models, building blocks, art materials, math manipulatives, and so forth (Vark, 2016).

This preference uses your experiences and the things that are real even when they are shown in pictures and on screens.

Students who have a strong **kinesthetic** preference for learning should use some or all of the following to **take in information:**

- all your senses – sight, touch, taste, smell, hearing
- laboratories
- field trips
- field tours
- examples of principles
- lecturers who give real-life examples
- applications
- hands-on approaches (computing)
- trial and error

> "Education is what survives when what has been learned has been forgotten."
>
> **–B. F. Skinner**

"Once you make a decision, the universe conspires to make it happen."

–Ralph Waldo Emerson

Dr. Covey believes that one must "seek first to understand, then to be understood." His research expressed the importance of "beginning with the end in mind." Based on the compelling research comprised in this chapter, one must consider the magnitude of the influence that building strong lasting relationships brings. I believe it's apparent that the Caucasian female teacher must strategically create opportunities to connect with the African American male student.

Non-Negotiable:

1. Raising teacher expectations
2. Increasing high time on task
3. Addressing blended learning and differentiation
4. Embedding daily active learning opportunities
5. Culturally responsive teaching

There are eight dimensions of Black culture, which are relevant to African American learning styles:

1. Movement and kinesthetic abilities developed
2. Value imagination and humor
3. Express feelings and language traditions

4. People oriented
5. Resourceful
6. View the whole, not separate pieces
7. Use inferences
8. Alert, curious, and good retention

When creating learning environments for African American students, critical thinking skills and some learning strategies are predictors of academic success:

- Learning in cooperative groups (Slavin, 1977)
- No reward system; intrinsic value only (Ladson-Billings, 1992)
- Supplementary after-school and weekend opportunities
- Using Black History Month to promote academic success and role models
- Parental involvement and knowledge about children and their learning

The test given to African American students being taught by African American teachers also indicates the lack of culture incorporated in the test based on the lack of success. One could conclude from this analogy that the assessment tool should be investigated further to include more test diversity. Listed below are a few recommendations to take inconsideration:

1. Definitions of learning styles and culture
2. Identify different learning styles

3. Study differences between African American and Caucasian students in critical thinking and learning styles
4. Avoid bias
5. Improve programs and break down cultural barriers

- Avoiding Bias:

  Teachers must avoid bias and understand that, regardless of cultural backgrounds, each student deserves to succeed

- An African American student's needs are different than those of the cultural mainstream
- Students are results of their culture
- Expand appreciation

Recognize and understand cultural differences and treat differences with respect

Intervene immediately
Value different experiences
Breaking Down Cultural Barriers

- Goal:
  - To learn about cultural differences in customs and beliefs to foster an atmosphere of trust, cross-cultural communication, and competence
  - To create insights, not stereotypes
  - To create cultural competence

Definitions of Learning Styles & Culture (Polce, 1987) defines learning style as "a way of perceiving, conceptualizing, and problem solving; a preferred way of interacting with and responding to the environment" (as cited in Willis 1992, p. 271).

Geertz defines culture as "an historically transmitted pattern of meanings employed in symbols, a system of inherited conceptions expressed in symbolic form by means of which men communicate, perpetuate, and develop their knowledge about attitudes towards life" (Comprehensive Multicultural Education, p.43).

Teachers, students, parents, and educators must become keenly aware of African American culture; learning the impact of culture on behavior, learning styles, and preferred teaching styles. The foundation teachers must appreciate is that there is a distinct effect culture has on learning style and as educators and parents we can facilitate the learning process by knowing the differences from culture to culture; thus directly affecting the learning styles and breaking down racial walls and teaching critical thinking skills.

CHAPTER SEVEN

Step One: Build Meaningful Relationships with African American Male Students

THE NON-NEGOTIABLE OF Educating African American Male Students begins with building relationships. Relationships are a part of life; we build relationships at home, at school, on our jobs, and in our communities. Relationships are very essential to our growth. However, building relationships that will last takes lots and lots of hard work, especially for some educators. I use the term some because not all educators struggle with building strong, positive, and productive healthy relationships with their students. There are, on the other hand, some who have difficulty building relationship with their colleagues as well as with students. Some teachers only see black or white, and I don't mean race. What I mean by this is that they don't use a common sense approach. You cannot deal with every personality the same way and each student has their own unique personality. What does this have to do with building healthy relationships? Everything.

In theory I try to employ a concept that comes from a biblical perspective and that is, *in order to have friends you must first show yourself to be friendly.* Oftentimes teachers try to enforce their rules without student's buy-in. I believe you have to allow students to be a part of the process. When you include students in the creation of your classroom rules and expectations they are more likely to follow them. This allows your students to believe you care enough to include them. Most students need to believe you care about them and respect them before they allow you to teach them. I know someone is reading this saying, "That's not my job; my job is to teach, not to become friends with students." Well, I'm not expecting you to hang out with students. I only expect you to project yourself as being friendly and to actually care about the number one reason you should have had for entered the teaching and learning profession in the first place: the love of students and the love of teaching them your special skill set. When educators enter the teaching profession for reasons other than the love of teaching and learning things becomes crunchy for all students, especially students of color. This is where things become very convoluted.

According to the Gallup Organization, people who have a best friend at work are seven times more likely to be engaged in their jobs. Wow, amazing! This is a very interesting concept to consider for the teacher and the student, especially when we look at the increase in group work as it relates to learning together. The report further indicates it doesn't have to be a best friend. Gallup found that people who simply have a good friend in the workplace are more likely to be satisfied. What if that term was changed from satisfied to successful and productive? Imagine how impactful a healthy and friendly student-teacher relationship can be. The Gallup report also indicates that human beings are naturally social creatures–we crave friendship and positive interactions just as we do food and water. So it makes sense that the better our relationships are at work, the happier and more productive we are. Good working relationships give us several other benefits; our work is more enjoyable when we have good relationships with those around us. Also, people are more likely to go along with changes that we want to implement, and we're more innovative and creative.

Understanding the art of building strong, positive relationships with students and parents are minimum expectations in all schools across the country. Although this is the basic standard expectation for private and public schools across our great nation there is still so much more work to do to make this a reality. In our schools today we are forced to focus on high stakes testing more so than on the nature vs. nurture aspects. Of course it's all extremely important and has to be performed consistently on a high level by all stakeholders. Most school scholars will recommend that you build strong, positive relationships will all of your parents and students. This sounds very practical but not always probable. What I mean by this is oftentimes as educators we reach out to our parents and students, perhaps the first week or day of school, but after that we drop the ball and rarely pick it back up until trouble comes. No parent wants to hear from the teacher, counselor, or administrator only when trouble comes. This process is normally successful with the classroom teacher if he or she has set a strong, firm foundation of trust and caring from day one with a phone call home to the parent. Normally on the first day there is no real reason to have a negative conversation with students or parents.

Educators have to develop or create opportunities to effectively communicate with their students each and every day. This begins with a simple greeting at the door once students arrive to class. Notice I haven't mentioned anything about race. Students only care about race based on your approach. Meaning if race doesn't affect you, it doesn't affect them. So at all costs, keep the main thing the main thing.

How to effectively communicate with students each and every day:

1. Begin with creating an opportunity to develop a one-on-one conversation with each student. This process should begin day one of the first day of the school year and progressively increase.
2. Compel students to have conversations with you about how to help them succeed in your class, other teachers' classes, or in life in general. I know you're busy but make the time. It's just that important.
3. Build trust between you and the student daily by being respectful, helpful, and caring. This goes a lot further than you would imagine.

4. Encourage them to be better than what they expect from themselves, parents, or society. Challenge them daily to improve by letting them know what's at stake.
5. Reinforce their level of greatness by seeing the glass as half filled, not half empty. Let them know how smart they are. Find something they do to build on and don't despise small beginnings.
6. Inspire them through loving your job and being the expert in your area of concentration. Make what you do relevant and real, and allow them to be able to see and feel your passion behind what you do.

"The secret in education relies in respecting the student."

–Author Unknown

7. Don't force them to learn you, you learn them. Create moments to learn where they are and where they would like to be. If they don't know and don't even have a clue, help them discover it!
8. Always believe in them no matter how they struggle or how often they struggle. Teach them to dig deeper within themselves and find a way to succeed.

9. Push them to limits that they have never been pushed to and 95 percent of the time they will meet or exceed the expectation. Then remove the limits.
10. Love them and treat them as your very own regardless of the difference in culture or ethnicity.

"Anyone who stops learning is old, whether at twenty or eighty. Anyone who keeps learning stays young."

–Henry Ford, Founder of Ford Motor Company

"Children must be taught how to think, not what to think."

–Margaret Mead

CHAPTER EIGHT

How Will Having More African American Male Teachers be Instrumental in Educating African American Males Students?

IF EDUCATORS LOCALLY, statewide, and nationwide are truly interested in closing the disparaging gaps for African American male students, the true answer begins with one of the seven habits of effective leaders by Dr. Covey. The habit I'm referencing is *seek first to understand, then to be understood.* Recruiting more African American males is the key. I strongly believe that former Secretary of Education Arne Duncan believed this philosophy and attempted to improve on the two percent population. He was very instrumental and vocal on the need to increase efforts to recruit and employ highly qualified African American male teachers, admin, and support.

When we reflect back on the information on the similar-to-me effect provided in the earlier chapters it only makes sense. Is this strategy going to give you the motivation you need? What are your thoughts?

Note: Thoughts based on this statement.

____

____

____

____

____

____

____

____

____

According to Dr. James Harris (2005), teachers, make up the bedrock of instructional activities for students. Harris, being a former principal and superintendent in various large school districts in the United States and Japan, believes that hiring highly qualified teachers is essential to all students' success. Harris demonstrated and documented this concept in his book, *10 Essential Strategies to Student Success.* The number one strategy a school system should employ is hiring highly qualified teachers. The reason is that the number one strategy stated in Dr. Harris' book is that teachers spend the bulk of their day working with students. Harris, being both a professor and mentor, has encouraged me as an educator. While cognizant of the African American male student dilemma in our country, Dr. Harris continues to break down barriers by reaching back and pulling African American students forward. Harris expresses the importance of pedagogy and demonstrates it in all his course offerings.

Note: Thoughts based on this statement.

____

____

____

____

____

____

____

____

____

Numerous scholars and commentators have argued that there is a growing disparity between the degree of racial/ethnic diversity in the nation's student population and the degree of diversity in the nation's elementary and secondary teaching force (Quiocho & Rios, 2000; Torres et al., 2004; Villegas & Lucas, 2004; Zumwalt & Craig, 2005). The National Council for Accreditation of Teacher Education first included "diversity" standards in 1976, which were later removed in 2006.

The nation's student body has changed drastically; however, the nation's teaching population has not. As indicated by Quiocho & Rios, there are several who argue that teachers have become less diverse and more homogeneously Caucasian. There are three arguments as to why increasing the racial/ethnic diversity of teachers would be beneficial. The demographic parity expresses the importance of minorities as excellent role models for all. According to Quiocho &

Rios, the racial/ethnic makeup of the teaching force should replicate that of the student population (Quiocho & Rios, 2000; Villegas & Lucas, 2004).

Note: Thoughts based on this statement.

____

____

____

____

____

____

____

____

____

Irvine (2002) indicates the importance of "cultural synchronicity" and its effect on the student population. He says the advantage of minority students being taught by minority teachers stems from "insider knowledge" based on having similar life experiences and cultural backgrounds (Villegas & Irvine, 2010). Research indicates that minority teachers are more likely than any non-minority candidates to seek employment in schools serving predominantly minority student populations, often in low-income, urban school districts (Foster, 1997; Ladson-Billings, 1995; Quiocho & Rios, 2000).

Note: Thoughts based on this statement.

____

____

____

____

____

____

____

____

____

Over the past several decades, organizations such as the Education Commission of the States (2003), the American Association of Colleges of Teacher Education (1993), and the National Educational Association (National Collaborative on Diversity in the Teaching Force, 2004) have advocated and implemented a wide range of initiatives designed to recruit minority candidates into teaching. These efforts have included future educator programs in high schools, partnerships between community colleges with higher minority student enrollments and four-year colleges with teacher education programs, career ladders for paraprofessionals already in the school system, and alternative certification programs (Clewell & Villegas, 1998).

Note: Thoughts based on this statement.

____

____

____

____

____

____

____

____

____

The Significance of Hiring African American Male Teachers

According to Arends' article on the significance of hiring African American male teachers, it's important to hire more African Americans because the public education system has changed education. The national population is forty-one percent minority and growing (National Center for Educational Statistics, 2005). However, the teaching profession has been unable to change (Arends, et al, 2000). Caucasian teachers remain at ninety percent while African Americans educators are at seven percent, and three percent of teachers are individuals of Hispanic and Asian backgrounds (National Center for Educational Statistics, 2005). Research indicates that African American male students account for ten percent of the total student population in America, but African American male teachers account for only two percent of the teaching profession (National Center for Educational Statistics, 2005).

Note: Thoughts based on this statement.

According to Brown's article entitled "Brothers Gonna Work It Out: Understanding the Pedagogic Performance of African American Male Teachers Working with African American Male Students," throughout most of the twentieth century, the question was less about just having a black teacher, but more about what kind of black teacher would provoke social and political changes. Brown indicated that by the late 1980s and early 1990s, there was a growing concern about the significance of culture to improve minority student achievement; several studies emerged regarding the pedagogical practices of the African American teacher (Foster, 1997; Irvine, 1990 a, b).

Note: Thoughts based on this statement.

____

____

____

____

____

____

____

____

____

A significant part of this research addressed the pedagogical skills aspects of the black teacher. Scholars have drawn from a variety of theoretical frameworks such as African-centered pedagogy (Irvine, 1990 a, b; & Ladson-Billings, 1995), Black feminism (Dixon, 2003), Black womanist thought (Beauboef-Lafontant, 2002, 2005), critical pedagogy (Ball, 2000), and critical race theory (Lynn, 2006) to illustrate the cultural and ideological dimensions of African American teacher performance. From the late 1980s to the present, three aspects of black teacher performance have been the focus: (1) verbal/rhetorical capacity; (2) social interactions; and (3) implicit and explicit use of cultural/political discourse (Foster, 1987, 1991 a, b, c, 1994, 1997; Howard, 2001; Irvine, 1990 a, b; King, 1991).

Note: Thoughts based on this statement.

____

____

____

____

____

____

____

____

____

According to Irvine, cultural responsive teachers employ a variety of speech acts such as "repetition, call and response, variation in pace, high emotional involvement, creative analogies, figurative language, vowel elongation, catch phrases, gestures and body movement (p. 60)." The other strategies are black teachers' social interaction with African American students (Irvine, 1990). Additionally, researchers note such interactions involve teachers' use of personal stories, joke telling, and dialect to help foster relationships with their students. Researchers also maintain black teachers employ a common political and cultural discourse in their practice. For example, some studies illustrate how African American teachers will regularly express to their students the political importance of education to their larger social and political worlds (Foster, 1997).

Note: Thoughts based on this statement.

____

____

____

____

____

____

____

____

____

According to Byron L. Daniel's research, *Evaluating Academic Achievement of African American Male Students in Guilford County, North Carolina Public Schools*, the home and the public school classroom have been key environments in the African American community and have been instrumental in developing identity and encouraging academic progress. Despite the dropout rates of African American males in secondary school, grades have increased while academic achievement scores in the primary grades have not. Daniel's research noted that the racial and gender composition of elementary school teachers did not match that of the students. This may contribute to the disproportionate achievement scores between African American and European American students (Daniels, 2010).

Note: Thoughts based on this statement.

____

____

____

____

____

____

____

____

____

Daniels' quantitative study examined the possible significant relationship between African American male teachers and the academic achievement of African American male students in Guilford County, North Carolina Public Schools using the Frequency Exact Test (Fischer's Exact Probability Test). The study compared six fifth-grade classroom's teachers: three with African American male teachers, three with European American male and female teachers, and African American female teachers, both of which had an average of four to nine African American male students in an average class of 20 to 30 students. The results could be used to assist in further evaluations of reasons for academic discrepancies. Potential solutions are discussed to decrease the achievement gap between African American youth and European American youth (Daniels, 2010).

Note: Thoughts based on this statement.

____

____

____

____

____

____

____

____

____

According to White's book, *Exclusion by Choice*, there are various reasons why African American males don't enter the teaching profession. These reasons include African American males' home lives, lack of opportunities, personal interactions while in school, and a lack of financial stability (White, 2009). African American males normally live in a single-family residence or in an abusive home (Passley, Gerring, & Gerson, 2006). According to Berger, living in single-family homes can be extremely damaging to a child, causing negative trends in daily practices: difficulty in focusing, stifled development, and the tendency to fall behind in school (Berger, 1994). As indicated by Staples, African American males have a tendency to earn low standardized tests scores, be placed in special education, experience suspension or expulsion, and drop out of school at a much higher rate than their Caucasian counterparts (Staples, 2010).

Note: Thoughts based on this statement.

As indicated by Anderson, African American males deal with so many challenges aside from failing in the classroom. For instance, African American males have to battle substance abuse, high unemployment rates, negative family situations, poverty, and incarceration (Anderson, 1999). As indicated by Ogbu (2002), African American males statistically rank lowest in the area of academic achievement, have the worst attendance, get suspended the most, and are expelled more often than their Caucasian counterparts. Also, African American males drop out of school and fail to pursue their Graduation Equivalency Diploma for various reasons (Pinkney, 2000; Roderick, 2003).

Note: Thoughts based on this statement.

____

____

____

____

____

____

____

____

According to Joyner, 72 percent of African American children are born to unwed mothers. The black community's 72 percent rate eclipses that of most other groups: 17 percent of Asians, 29 percent of whites, 53 percent of Hispanics and 66 percent of Native Americans were born to unwed mothers in 2008, the most recent year for which government figures are available. The rate for the overall U.S. population was 41 percent. This issue entered the public consciousness in 1965, when a now famous government report by future senator Daniel Patrick Moynihan described a "tangle of pathology" among blacks who fed a 24 percent black "illegitimacy" rate. The white rate then was four percent (Joyner, 2010). In essence, failure to complete high school requirements will negate post-secondary success and forfeit opportunities to receive degrees in education or in any field of study (Pinkney, 2000; Roderick, 2003).

Note: Thoughts based on this statement.

African American males have had very poor experiences in school. For instance, Staples indicated that African American males suffer being reprimanded and embarrassed by their teachers at a much higher rate than Caucasian males. According to Staples, African American males are severely mistreated in the public school (Staples, 2010). Motivating African American males to enter the teaching profession is challenging with regard to the various other professions. As indicated by Pinkney & Rodrick (2003), teaching is not a job that people enter because of the money. Teaching, unlike other professions, does not offer large salaries. People who choose teaching as a profession often choose based on some moral commitment of giving back to society.

Note: Thoughts based on this statement.

According to the HR Reported data, the annual salary for someone with the job title of an elementary school teacher may vary depending on a number of factors including location, years of experience, and level of education. For example, the median expected annual pay for a typical elementary school teacher in the United States is $53,430, so 50 percent of the people who perform the job of an elementary school teacher in the United Sates are expected to make less than $53,430 (HR Reported data as of June 2014). As indicated by Eitle & Eitle (2002), money is one of the number one contributing factors individuals take into consideration when choosing a career.

Note: Thoughts based on this statement.

____

____

____

____

____

____

____

____

According to Eitle & Eitle, African American males who live in poverty or below their means typically prefer to pursue careers geared towards sports. Unlike Caucasian families, African American males' families encourage them to participate in sports at a much greater rate (Spence, 2000). As indicated by Griffith, this is the reason we see African American males seeking to identify themselves based on their athletic talents. African American males find validation with sports because sports are encouraged at home (Griffith, 2007). Powell indicated that African American males put very little emphasis on academics in comparison to sports (Powell, 2008, p. 73)

Note: Thoughts based on this statement.

____

____

____

____

____

____

____

____

____

According to Harrison & Lampman, African American males become extremely disappointed when they don't end up with careers in sports. Harrison & Lampman indicated that because of the negative behavior African American males see their sports heroes demonstrate through the media and on television, they too become victims of such negative and destructive behaviors, such as drug abuse. This negative behavior comes after they have placed so much emphasis on pursing sports as a career and fail (Harrison & Lampman, 2001). According to Cherry, the social cognitive and sociocultural theories play a very important part as to why African American males don't enter the teaching profession. Cherry indicated that one of the leading reasons why African American males don't enter the teaching profession is because African American males learn by watching.

Note: Thoughts based on this statement.

____

____

____

____

____

____

____

____

____

As indicated by Cherry, this is called the social cognitive ideology (Cherry, 2010). Day to day events can have a huge impact on an individual's opinion about life. If a student's life is filled with drugs or abuse is prevalent, then the possibility exists he could model himself after the events of the environment, and for children, it's sometimes difficult to differentiate good from bad (Cherry, 2010). Cherry indicated that dysfunction could prevent a child from knowing and understanding what is socially acceptable and cause African American males to choose paths that do not lead to teaching.

Note: Thoughts based on this statement.

____

____

____

____

____

____

____

____

____

Bianco, Leech, & Mitchell's, article *Pathways to Teaching: African American Male Teens Explore Teaching as a Career* outlines pathways to teaching African American teens to explore becoming teachers. The focal points of the article include information on the scarcity of African American male teachers, research findings, and a description of a pre-collegiate course designed to encourage high school students of color, including African American males, to explore teaching. The research presented in this article draws from survey and interview data. Bianco, Leech, & Mitchell, examine factors that influence 11th and 12th grade African American males' consideration of teaching careers and explore the impact of a pre-collegiate pathway to teaching program. "The results of the study on *Pathways to Teaching: African American Male Teens Explore Teaching as a Career* exposed the complexity of effective recruitment while also demonstrating how a successful program has the capacity to encourage young African American males to reframe their thinking and see themselves as potential future teachers." (Bianco, Leech, & Mitchell, 2011; *The Journal of Negro Education* 2011, 368-383).

Note: Thoughts based on this statement.

____
____
____
____
____
____
____
____
____

Byrd, Butler, Lewis, Bonner, Rutledge, & Watson's 2011 research study titled *Identifying New Sources of African American Male Pre-service Teachers* examined the experience of one African American former college athlete and two athletic department academic advisors at BCS Division University in the southern region of the United States. The study was based on the African American male K-12 teacher shortage. The participants of the study were interviewed to examine the experience of student athletes as they relate to exposure to teaching as a possible profession early in their academic career. Retrospective interviews were used. Key themes that emerged from this study were incorrect advising of student athletes, perceptions of the academic structure of teacher education, and exposing student athletes to possible careers. Recommendations for practice based on the data from this study were made to generate a pathway from student-athlete to student-teacher in big-time college athletic programs.

Note: Thoughts based on this statement.

____

____

____

____

____

____

____

____

____

Graham & Erwin's article entitled, *I Don't Think Black Men Teach Because of How They Get Treated as Students: High-Achieving African American Boys' Perceptions of Teaching as a Career Option* indicated that the teaching profession is viewed as negative and not a viable career option by high-achieving high school-aged African American males.

Note: Thoughts based on this statement.

CHAPTER NINE

Qualitative Phenomenological Research Study on Motivating African American Males to Enter the Education Profession

BY CONDUCTING A Qualitative Phenomenological Research Study on Motivating African American Males to Enter the Education Profession (Bolar, Lawrence, 2015) we discovered very important data concerning African American males and the education profession. The study consisted of presenting ten questions centered specifically on motivating African American males to enter the profession, to African American males who were currently working in the profession. The interview questions were asked individually at separate times. The questions and results of the study are below.

Interview Questions/Results

1. What are your thoughts on the current status of the elementary educational profession as it pertains to African American male educators?
   A. Need more 13/13 B. Don't need more 0/15

2. What influenced you to select the field of education as your desired profession?
   A. Self-motivated 5/13 B. Wanted to give back 7/13

3. What was your personal motivation to enter the elementary teaching profession?
   A. Self-Motivation 13/13 B. Motivated by someone else 0/13

4. What impact did salary play in your decision to enter the elementary teaching profession?
   A. No impact 13/13 B. Impact 0/13

5. Describe any barriers you have faced entering the elementary education profession?
   A. No barriers 5/13 B. Barriers 8/13

6. In your experience has any person or persons expressed their perception of your profession as feminine or as women's work? Please explain.
   A. Women's work 2/13 B. Not women's work 13/13

7. Describe your experience as an African American male teacher working in a female dominated profession?
   A. Non challenging 4/13 B. Challenging 9/13

8. Illustrate a time where you felt any bias or prejudices as an African American male in your school or school division.
   A. No bias 13/13 B. Bias 0/13

9. There have been wide ranging debates about the belief of African American male teachers having a positive impact on the academic performance of African American male students. What are your thoughts on this theory?
   A. Positive impact 13/13 B. No Positive Impact 0/13

10. Do you believe as an African American male that your school division has provided enough support for attracting and retaining African American male teachers? Please explain.
   A. Have 6/13 B. Have Not 7/13

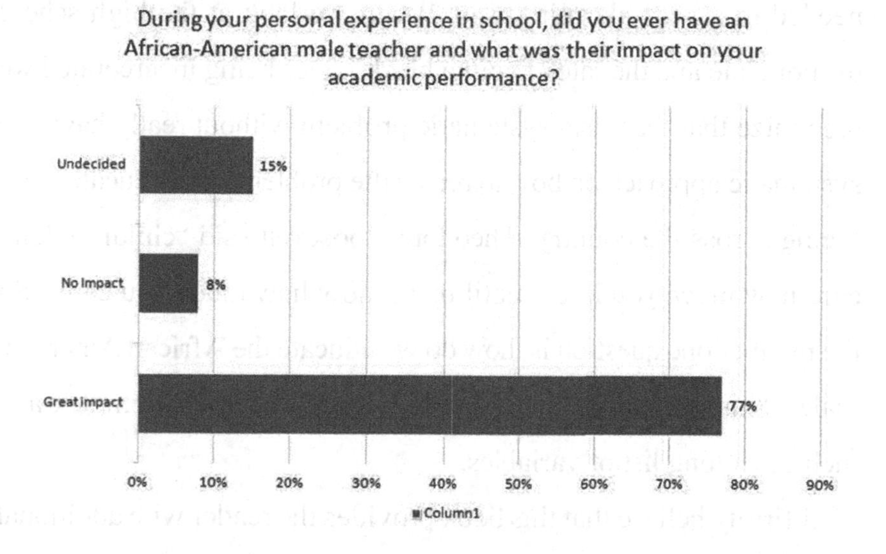

The research also indicates that 15 percent of the participants state that money would be the best way to increase recruitment; 23 percent state that positive exposure and money would have the greatest impact; 62 percent state that providing continued positive exposure would be their advice for strengthening, recruiting, and retaining African American males in the elementary teaching profession.

CHAPTER TEN

NCLB: A Problem or Solution?

EDUCATING AFRICAN AMERICAN males has become a real challenge and the non-negotiable of educating African American males are needed in a very alarming way. When we look at the high school dropout rate and the rate of young black males being incarcerated we recognize that there is a systematic problem without really having a systematic approach on how to repair the problems that educators are facing across the country. Theodore Roosevelt said "children don't care how much you know until they know how much you care." So the number one question is, how do we educate the African American male? This question sounds simple but it's extremely complex and includes a long list of variables.

I firmly believe that this book provides the reader with additional resources that promote and cultivate the successful educating of African American males. I believe that one of the reasons for the challenge that exists is because 72 percent of African American children are born to unwed mothers. One has to take this data into account when seeking novel ways to educate African American males. When we look at the family structure we see that there is a huge disparity facing African American males being reared in homes that are unbalanced. This lack of balance comes from being raised in fatherless homes and in some cases having no relationship with their father. When we look at the alarming rates of incarcerated African American males we can also attribute this to the challenge of educating a young man who may not have encountered a father figure to encourage him to do well in society or school, and just having no one in general to identify with.

This becomes more problematic when we see the numbers are nationwide. With the charter school approach focusing on at-risk, behavioral-based problems such as low graduation rates, and high dropout rates, we see an emerging trend.

The No Child Left Behind Act essentially uncovered a large percentage of these disparities unintentionally through data. My research includes various captivating topics such as Teaching African American Male Students, examining instructional methods, and cultural differences. The objective for sharing this data is to ensure with fidelity that no child is left behind. Based on this research, my recommendation would indicate that cultural responsive initiatives should be included in every school's curriculum framework. This recommendation will help service administrators, teachers, school counselors, social workers, and colleges or universities producing future educators.

This chapter has unveiled the way the NCLB act uncovered how African American Males have been allowed to disconnect and underachieve without any real reform being instituted until now. The

No Child Left Behind Act of 2001 (NCLB) is a United States Act of Congress that is a reauthorization of the Elementary and Secondary Education Act, which included Title I, the government's flagship aid program for disadvantaged students. NCLB supports standards-based education reform based on the premise that setting high standards and establishing measurable goals can improve individual outcomes in education. The Act requires states to develop assessments in basic skills. To receive federal school funding, states must give these assessments to all students at select grade levels. The Act does not assert a national achievement standard. Each individual state develops their own standards. NCLB expanded the federal role in public education through annual testing, annual academic progress, report cards, teacher qualifications, and funding changes. The bill passed in the U.S. Congress with bipartisan support.

The legislation was proposed by President George W. Bush on January 23, 2001. It was coauthored by Representatives John Boehner (R-OH), George Miller (D-CA), and Senators Edward Kennedy (D-MA) and Judd Gregg (R-NH). The United States House of Representatives passed the bill on May 23, 2001 (voting 384–45), and the United States Senate passed it on June 14, 2001 (voting 91–8). President Bush signed it into law on January 8, 2002.

Increased Accountability

Supporters of the NCLB claim one of the strong positive points of the bill is the increased accountability that is required of schools and teachers. According to the legislation, schools must pass yearly tests that judge student improvement over the fiscal year. These yearly standardized tests are the main means of determining whether schools live up to required standards. If required improvements are not made, the schools face decreased funding and other punishments that contribute to the increased accountability. According to supporters, these goals help teachers and schools realize the significance and importance of the educational system and how it affects the nation. Opponents of this law say that the punishments only hurt the schools and do not contribute to the improvement of student education.

In addition to and in support of the above points, proponents claim that No Child Left Behind:

- Links state academic content standards with student outcomes.
- Measures student performance: a student's progress in reading and math must be measured annually in grades 3 through 8 and at least once during high school via standardized tests.
- Provides information for parents by requiring states and school districts to give parents detailed report cards on schools and districts explaining the school's AYP performance. Schools must also inform parents when their child is being taught by a teacher or para-professional who does not meet "highly qualified" requirements.
- Establishes the foundation for schools and school districts to significantly enhance parental involvement and improved

administration through the use of the assessment data to drive decisions on instruction, curriculum and business practices.

The state of Pennsylvania has proposed tying teachers' salaries to test scores. If a district's students do poorly, the state cuts the district's budget the following year and the teachers get a pay cut. Critics point out that if a school does poorly, taking funds away from its budget and cutting teacher salaries will likely hamper the school's ability to improve.

The act requires schools to rely on scientifically based research for programs and teaching methods. The act defines this as "research that involves the application of rigorous, systematic, and objective procedures to obtain reliable and valid knowledge relevant to education activities and programs." Scientifically based research results in "replicable and applicable findings" from research that used appropriate methods to generate persuasive, empirical conclusions.

Non-scientific methods include following tradition, personal preferences, and non-scientific research, such as research based on case studies, ethnographies, personal interviews, discourse analysis, grounded theory, action research, and other forms of qualitative research. These are generally not an acceptable basis for making decisions about teaching children under the act.

Quality and Distribution of Teachers

Prior to the NCLB act, new teachers were typically required to have a bachelor's degree, be fully certified, and demonstrate subject matter knowledge—generally through tests. Under NCLB, existing teachers, including those with tenure, were also supposed to meet standards. They could meet the same requirements set for new teachers, or could meet a state-determined "...high, objective, uniform state standard of evaluation," a.k.a. HOUSSE. Downfall to the quality requirements of the NCLB legislation have received little research attention, in part because state rules require few changes from pre-existing practice. There is also little evidence that the rules have altered trends in observable teacher traits.

Criticisms of Standardized Testing Under NCLB

Critics argue that the focus on standardized testing (all students in a state take the same test under the same conditions) encourages teachers to teach a narrow subset of skills that the teacher believes increases test performance, rather than focus on deeper understanding of the overall curriculum. For example, if the teacher knows that all of the questions on a math test are simple addition problems (e.g., What is 2 + 3?), then the teacher might not invest any class time on the practical applications of addition so that there is more time for the material which is assessed on the test. This is colloquially referred to as "teaching to the test." "Teaching to the test" has been observed to raise test scores, though not as much as other teaching techniques.

Many teachers who practice "teaching to the test" misinterpret the educational outcomes the tests are designed to measure. On two state tests (New York State and Michigan) and the National

Assessment of Educational Progress (NAEP) almost two-thirds of eighth graders missed math word problems that required an application of the Pythagorean theorem to calculate the distance between two points. The teachers correctly anticipated the content of the tests, but incorrectly assumed each test would present simplistic items rather than well-constructed, higher-order items.

Inconsistencies and poor planning in test administration may have violated the Individuals with Disabilities Education Act (IDEA), which states that schools must accommodate disabled students. For example, it is normally acceptable for teachers to read test questions aloud to visually impaired students. However, scores were once invalidated (reported as zeros) for a group of blind students because the testing protocol did not specifically allow teachers or aides to read the test questions to the students. Although it may not matter, as the NCLB ACT was passed after IDEA, and may therefore override it where they differ.

Some people oppose the use of standardized testing, or any type of testing, to determine educational quality. They prefer alternatives such as teacher opinions, classwork, and performance-based assessments.

Some also argue that NCLB testing is negative for non-English-language immersion schools, particularly those that immerse students in Native American languages, many of which are endangered and in critical need of new speakers. Native students who learn in their heritage languages have lower dropout rates and higher academic achievement than those who learn in English, yet NCLB requires even very young students to take standardized tests in English, disrupting the immersion environment of these schools that is crucial for student success.

Under No Child Left Behind, schools were held almost exclusively accountable for absolute levels of student performance. But that meant that even schools that were making great strides with students were still labeled as "failing" just because the students had not yet made it all the way to a "proficient" level of achievement. Since 2005, the U.S. Department of Education has approved 15 states to implement growth model pilots. Each state adopted one of four distinct growth models: Trajectory, Transition Tables, Student Growth Percentiles, and Projection.

The incentives for improvement also may cause states to lower their official standards. Because each state can produce its own standardized tests, a state can make its statewide tests easier to increase scores. Missouri, for example, improved testing scores but openly admitted that they lowered the standards. 2007 study by the U.S. Dept. of Education indicates that the observed differences in states' reported scores is largely due to differences in the stringency of their standards.

Quality of Education

- Increases the quality of education by requiring schools to improve their performance
- Improves quality of instruction by requiring schools to implement "scientifically based research" practices in the

classroom, parent involvement programs, and professional development activities for those students that are not encouraged or expected to attend college.

- Supports early literacy through the Early Reading First initiative.
- Emphasizes reading, language arts, mathematics, and science achievement as "core academic subjects."

Effects on Racial and Ethnic Minority Students

Attention to minority populations seeks to narrow the class and racial achievement gap in the United States by creating common expectations for all. NCLB has shown mixed success in eliminating the racial achievement gap. Although test scores are improving, they are improving equally for all races, which mean that minority students are still behind whites.

Requires schools and districts to focus their attention on the academic achievement of traditionally under-served groups of children, such as low-income students, students with disabilities, and students of "major racial and ethnic subgroups". Each state is responsible for defining major racial and ethnic subgroups itself. Many previous state-created systems of accountability measured only average school performance—so schools could be highly rated even if they had large achievement gaps between affluent and disadvantaged students.

State refusal to produce non-English assessments All students who are learning English have an automatic three-year window to take assessments in their native language, after which they must normally demonstrate proficiency on an English-language assessment. However, the local education authority may grant an exception to any individual English learner for another two years' testing in his or her native language on a case-by-case basis.

In practice, however, only 10 states choose to test any English language learners in their native language (almost entirely Spanish speakers). The vast majority of English language learners are given English language assessments.

Many schools test or assess students with limited English proficiency even when the students are exempt from NCLB-mandated reporting, because the tests may provide useful information to the teacher and school. In certain schools with large immigrant populations, this exemption comprises a majority of young students.

Demographic study of AYP failure rates and requirement for failing schools One study found that schools in California and Illinois that have not met AYP serve 75–85 percent minority students while schools meeting AYP have less than 40 percent minority students. Schools that do not meet AYP are required to offer their students' parents the opportunity to transfer their students to a non-failing school within the district, but it is not required that the other school accepts the student. NCLB controls the portion of federal Title I funding based upon each school meeting annual set standards. Any participating school that does not make Adequate Yearly Progress (AYP) for two years must offer parents the choice to send their child to a non-failing school in the district, and after three years, must provide supplemental services, such as free tutoring or after-school assistance. After five years of not meeting AYP, the school must make dramatic changes to how the school is run, which could entail state-takeover.

Rigor Relevance Relationship

In recent years we have seen a phenomenological shift in education and closure brought to the No Child Left Behind Act that was instituted by President George W. Bush. The act brought about a paradigm shift that has led to many educational reforms. A large percentage of this school reform has been centered around the African American student population with a laser-like focus on African American males. This central focus has caused an increase in the importance of understanding cultural and incorporating it into the daily teaching and learning process.

Cultural Responsive Teaching Survey

1. What is cultural responsive teaching?
2. How do you incorporate culture in your daily lesson plan?
3. How can we build vocabulary around culture? Example: Compare and contrast three words our students can use to change over dialect a.k.a. code switch. Example: To bank a student could mean to have a physical altercation with more than one student. Example: Discombobulated vs. confused.

4. How do your students feel about your content area? Do they like or dislike it?
5. Give your definition of the following in your opinion. What is rigor? What is relevance? What is relationship?

How to Incorporate Culture In Your Daily Lesson Plan

The first step to incorporating culture in your lesson plan begins with the teacher performing an environment scan of his or her classroom. An environmental scan is an assessment of the students and their strengths. Performing an environmental scan will provide the teacher with the opportunity to obtain additional knowledge and resources about their classroom and the students they are serving.

1. Perform an environmental scan of the classroom.
2. Set clear and precise expectations.
3. Inspect what you expect.
4. Create opportunities to build relationships.
5. High time on task.
6. Don't allow students to disconnect or check out.

Purpose and Process

Optimize student learning

Common purpose

Performance indicator

CHAPTER ELEVEN

Listen Up: African American Male Educators Speak About Their Educational Experiences During K-12 Life and After

FOUR EMERGING THEMES were revealed through the course of the data analysis. These emerging themes were revealed as common phrases and statements consistently mentioned by the participants, and can be used to create generalizations about the phenomena. The four emerging themes were: (a) promotion of the profession, (b) monetary/financial incentives, (c) desire to help others, and (d) community support.

Detailed Interview Results

1. **What are your thoughts on the current status of the elementary educational profession as it pertains to African American male educators?**

AAME#1 He believes there is a lack of males in the profession and that most African American males who are former athletes only want to go into P.E., where there is no Standard of Learning (SOL) requirement.

AAME#2 His thoughts are that we need to increase the number of African American males in all school systems, especially in Petersburg where males need good roles to follow as well as examples of what a man should be.

AAME#3 He believes that African American males are set up for failure. Public school education has been only geared toward SOL testing. Focusing on SOLs don't allow you to focus on a student; it's more robotic than it once was. He also believes the teacher exam keeps African American males out of the profession based on their failure to pass the teacher exam. African American males graduate from college in May and need to get a job. Most African Americans can't wait to hear the result of the test because they have to get a job right away. They don't have anyone to depend on or to support them until test scores return so they take jobs in other professions.

AAME#4 He believes that the profession is lacking. He is a graduate from the local university but he feels like college students don't want to stick around the area.

AAME#5 He believes there aren't enough African American males in the education profession. This lack of African American males impacts the number of role models and ultimately affects society's perception of African American males.

AAME#6 He believes that there need to be a lot more African American educators, especially in elementary.

AAME#7 He has worked in the same building for nine years and has only seen one other African American male in the building.

AAME#8 He believes that it is important that we get more African American males into the profession because the youth will benefit from it.

AAME#9 He feels like we do need more African American males who have a large demographic of African American students.

AAME#10 He believes that the elementary education has improved since he started 18 years ago but not a whole lot.

AAME#11 He believes the profession needs more African American males, because if the number doesn't increase there will be more African American males going into the prison system. The students need to see more African American male teachers to become exposed to positive role models.

2. What influenced you to select the field of education as your desired profession?

AAME#1 His football coach inspired him to want to go into education because his coach would pick him up and take him to practice. During his rides to practice the coach would tell him about life and how important it was to make good use of his time, especially with his family. His coach explained to him that once he goes home he has to be dad and husband instead of teacher. So he learned the importance of time management and getting everything done before he leaves work so he can be a father once he got home. His coach was a Caucasian male who still coaches today.

AAME#2 The participant has always had a knack for leadership and a desire to give back to the community through the kids because the kids are our future.

AAME#3 He loves teaching students and he does adjunct work at VSU. He feels it's best to catch them while they are young.

AAME#4 All for the call of duty, he is a military guy and in having conversations he always had a connection with younger students. He was always able to calm students down. He has had three tours oversees in the military and feels like he is the right person for the job.

AAME#5 He appreciates having the opportunity to work with students in general that need help and enjoys giving back to students who are less fortunate. The desire to give back as a sense of duty motivates him to pay it forward in his own community.

AAME#6 He has always wanted to be a teacher but didn't know what he wanted to teach. He selected elementary because he would have the opportunity to teach all subjects.

AAME#7 He found himself tutoring and as a kid he worked in the library at Howard University.

AAME#8 He knew from the time he was in high school that he would go into education. He believed that if he went into elementary more opportunities would be available.

AAME#9 He had a desire to coach baseball and decided to go into education.

AAME#10 He is in the business of helping people and likes seeing kids learn new information.

AAME#11 The participant began his career working in the field of corrections and saw so many African American males coming into the prison system that as a result he wanted to make a difference and decided to enter the education profession.

3. **What was your personal motivation to enter the elementary teaching profession?**

AAME#1 The participant believes that growing up going to vacation Bible school as a child helped influence him. He likes the idea of being his own boss and doesn't want anyone to tell him how to get the job done as long as he can get the expected outcome.

AAME#2 The participant has a strong desire to mold children to create a better future for us all.

AAME#3 He believes if you catch students early you can develop the learning skills because student soak up information quickly.

AAME#4 He has always had a unique ability to connect with younger children and believes that the foundation begins while children are at a young age. He feels like you should not have to water down life lessons to students.

AAME#5 Working in Maryland with students with various abilities and disabilities was an eye opening experience for him. The participant started out in speech pathology. This opened up the opportunity to deal with all races of students.

AAME#6 He has a background in music and was going to go into the music field but decided that music was too rigorous. His next thought was to be a music teacher.

AAME#7 He began working with 5th grade students in a private setting. He was working in the middle school and was looking for a job and landed a one working on the elementary level.

AAME#8 His uncle is a science teacher on the high school level and he wanted his family to be proud of him for choosing education. He really enjoys the feedback he receives from his students each day.

AAME#9 He began working in elementary education because it allowed him the ability to get more involved with the coaching aspect, and because there were no openings in his first choice, the high school level.

AAME#10 He chose elementary based on his 3rd grade experience, which was a negative one. He had a teacher that would run her class ring into the back of all the students' heads. He didn't like it and wanted to become a teacher so they could be exposed to more caring and positive educators.

AAME#11 The participant's mother and sister are retired educators who wrote really well and communicate well, and they instilled this in him.

4. What impact did salary play in your decision to enter the elementary teaching profession?

AAME#1 After graduation he was unemployed and prayed that the Lord would give him a job to be an independent man. Salary had no determination on his decision to enter the elementary education profession.

AAME#2 Salary did not play a role in his decision-making process. There were jobs that paid more money, however, the opportunity to enter a professional field where he could make an impact in his community was most appealing to him.

AAME#3 Salary had no impact on his decision to go into education.

AAME#4 Salary had no impact at all. He does wish he made more money but it did not impact his decision.

AAME#5 In the beginning there was no impact until he started a family. He just liked what he was doing. He looked for opportunities to increase his finances so he could stay in the educational profession.

AAME#6 Salary played no impact on his decision. He looked more at more at the commitment and the personal and professional rewards.

AAME#7 Salary did not play a role, however, it was an increase coming from the private teaching setting.

AAME#8 Salary had no impact; he says that everyone knows there is not great pay in education and that you have to do it for the right reasons.

AAME#9 In his case salary had a positive impact based on what he was making at his previous job. It was a pay increase and the hours were better.

AAME#10 Salary had no impact on his decision.

AAME#11 Salary had no impact on his decision to enter the profession.

5. Describe any barriers you have faced entering the elementary education profession.

AAME#1 The biggest hurdle he faced was being young. He graduated in May 2005 and started working in September 2005. People he worked with were afraid of change. Working as a special education teacher, he did not get the support he needed to be successful because he was looked at as a disciplinary figure as supposed to an educator. The ladies he worked with mostly wanted him to pull out students because they were a behavior problem.

AAME#2 The barriers are twofold: the first is the salary and the second is that in elementary you have to have the ability to balance a strong demeanor with the nurturing quality when working with young children, especially in lower grades.

AAME#3 The teacher exam was his only barrier.

AAME#4 He has not had any barriers and the process has been fairly easy due to his decision to go to the military first.

AAME#5 He had no problem getting a job directly out of college. As an African American male it was really easy to get a job because there were not many African Americans in the profession. He believes that due to the underrepresentation this is still true today.

AAME#6 The only barriers were financial barriers in college. The testing was not a major issue for him.

AAME#7 He didn't have any barriers. The practice exam was a challenge but he always knew he could pass the test.

AAME#8 He used to wear cornrows (braids) as his hairstyle of choice, however, his school made him cut his hair to do student teaching. In the place where he did his student teaching the students were predominantly white. The school only had one minority teacher and she was of a mixed race different from his. He believes the majority of the people in the school didn't like him being there. His university pulled him out of the student teaching capacity as a result of his experience there and sent him to a predominantly black school to complete his student teaching. He states that there was a constant comparison to white universities in relations to the student teaching experience in his first school. He felt awkward based on these comparisons since he was coming from a HBCU. He had no problem passing his test and passed it the first time.

AAME#9 He wasn't certified when he began so he was told by central office personnel that he couldn't even get an interview.

AAME#10 He stated that as a male figure you get it hard from students who don't have a male in the home environment. He believes that a lot of students see negative images outside of school and as a result believe that they will be treated the same way in school.

AAME#11 He expressed that he didn't have any real barriers, he took the teacher exam and passed the writing portion but he finally took the VCLA and passed it.

6. **In your experience has any person or persons expressed their perception of your profession as feminine or as women's work? Please explain.**

AAME#1 In his first assignment he had to work with several students who were in wheelchairs and nonverbal. He had to change diapers so people did look at him and what he was doing as feminine work.

AAME#2 Usually as a desired commodity in the elementary school setting, there have been times when a female-dominated administration was or seemed to be inequitable when assigning challenging students.

AAME#3 He has never experienced being looked at as someone who does women's work.

AAME#4 He has heard sly comments in the military environment but nowhere else.

AAME#5 He has not experienced this perception and believes it is because people see that there is a need to have more African American male role models in the lives' of the students.

AAME#6 He doesn't recall a time where anyone has made any negative comments to him about being a male educator.

AAME#7 He said yes and that people have had that perception because stereotypically women are the nurturers. He said you don't normally see male influence until you get to the upper level.

AAME#8 He has not had an issue with this, however, people think his job is easy and believe all he has to do is sit in the class with kids.

AAME#9 He said yes and no. Some of his personal friends give him a hard time because they have different professions, such as labor jobs.

AAME#10 The participant has never experienced this.

AAME#11 No, he has never had this happen.

7. **Describe your experience as an African American male teacher working in a female dominated profession.**

AAME#1 He has been asked to do everything from painting to handy work—anything that requires a male. If it is raining outside and the female staff doesn't want to get their hair wet he is asked to do it. The male custodian doesn't come in until after 2 p.m. so he is always asked to do any work that is typically considered men's work.

AAME#2 He stated that 80 percent of the females that he has worked with would rather have a male supervisor or team leader as opposed to a female leader. Based on his experiences, it appears that there is a higher expectation of leadership for African American males in the elementary education profession.

AAME#3 He doesn't have any problems but feels that there have been experiences where he is the person who has to do the heavy lifting. Also, there are some things that he allows them to say to him that a female wouldn't accept from a male.

AAME#4 He feels that it is okay. He normally gets acclimated quickly but has not gelled as quickly with the females. He does feel he needs to develop some cohesiveness and has been told it's good to have a male around.

AAME#5 He said the experience is different but that you learn to blend in. He stated that you learn not to be a feminist and that you learn to respect those who work with you just as they learn to respect you. He was the only male for eight years working in the building. He is often asked to offer an opinion from a male prospective.

AAME#6 Most of the experiences are positive although often in meetings the principal forgets to say "he" or "him." Recently the bathroom has become an issue because the females use both bathrooms. But most of his encounters are positive.

AAME#7 He was the only African American male working in his building beside the two custodians. The experience didn't bother him at all until someone mentioned it.

AAME#8 He says the experience has its pros and cons and that women can be more moody. He believes that because they have been inferior for so long they try to push their authority.

AAME#9 He says it required an adjustment working with a female-dominated group based on their emotions and how their emotions come into play so often. He feels that wouldn't be the case if more males were in the profession.

AAME#10 He stated that at first it takes some getting used to but once you get comfortable with it it's just like any other job.

AAME#11 He tries to get along with everyone whether they're a female or male. If he has a problem he goes to the person and addresses them directly.

8. **Define your greatest reward as an African American male working in elementary education.**

AAME#1 Seeing his former and present students adjust their behavior if they are doing something wrong in his presence. They will pull up their pants, stop smoking, or anything that they may be doing wrong, out of respect for him.

AAME#2 The success of any of his students is a great joy, however, to see a young black male that he has supported excel in education brings the greatest reward.

AAME#3 Seeing a student who excels, graduates, and goes on to college is his greatest achievement and he enjoys seeing them when he is out in the community.

AAME#4 The response of the African American male student. He feels that it is so rewarding to see how the students want to get to know you and respect you. Speaking properly and having manners are some of the ways his black student reflect his example.

AAME#5 The participant's greatest reward is working with students and family and seeing them become successful. He believes that when working with African American males their parents seem to trust you more.

AAME#6 The greatest reward is being different based on his teaching style. He tries to make his classroom experience more positive based on him being the only African American teacher.

AAME#7 seeing the children grow physically and intellectually.

AAME#8 Seeing the light bulb turn on in the minds of his students when they learn new material. He believes with his students he has set a strong foundation for the future of America.

AAME#9 His greatest reward was working in a community that he grew up in and mentoring in his community, where you don't see a lot of positive African Americans. He wants males to look up to him as well as the professional sports figures and entertainers.

AAME#10 His greatest reward is seeing his former students being successful and knowing that he or she has made it in society.

AAME#11 Seeing his former students being successful and the students recognizing him as being instrumental in their success.

9. **Describe your greatest challenge as an African American male working in elementary.**

AAME#1 Being looked upon as Mr. Fix It. As the only male teacher in the content area he is looked upon to fix everything, from fights to covering a class for someone to go to the bathroom. He is expected to have to be able to relate to every male student regardless of his relationship or lack of relationship with the student and finds this unrealistic.

AAME#2 The greatest challenge is raising student expectations to the point that no child feels educationally inferior.

AAME#3 The greatest challenge is to get his voice across to certain female professionals. He feels like females have more compassion where men don't.

AAME#4 Earning the respect of the female students. They seem to have a harder time following the rules from an African American male teacher.

AAME#5 The greatest challenge is getting the family involved. Many families have burned bridges with the school and as a result have trust issues with the school.

AAME#6 Staff often uses him way too much because the males are not behaving in the female teachers' classrooms most of the times.

AAME#7 As a special educator, finding the weaknesses or the intelligence in the child to help them grow where they can shine and best access the knowledge they need to be successful. Believes time plays a critical role as well and he is an advocate for year-round school.

AAME#8 He believes that most of the time he gets most of the troubled kids because he is a male. He believes that students listen to him more because he is a man.

AAME#9 His greatest challenge is being taken seriously. Some people don't feel like he is capable to respond intelligently as a male. There appears to be a low level of expectations of him as a male and especially since he works in P.E.

AAME#10 Working with students whose father left and never came back.

AAME#11 The greatest challenge is accepting negative behavior that you, as a teacher, have to tolerate.

10. Please share one memorable experience with your students as an African American male classroom teacher, positive or negative. Share one example of your experience working with your students' parents as an African American male teacher. How has it challenged you and strengthened you as an educator?

AAME#1 His greatest reward is taking students on trips seeing the response of the students being outside their environment. He realized many of his students had never been outside Petersburg, VA. The students thought they were in D.C. only traveling to Richmond, VA. As a student advocate he has had good relationships with his students' parents and these positive interactions with parents have strengthened him and allowed him to gain parent support.

AAME#2 As an African American male working in an elementary setting, he found that African American males were stereotyped as being able to handle the most extreme disciplinary behaviors; consequently, as a teacher, he would ultimately receive the majority of the overage students—students with behavior problems, and an increased number of students with emotional disabilities.

AAME#3 In his experience, working with a student who has never been toilet trained after other school districts never took the time to help the student. His mother took the time to share with him that he was the only one who took the time to toilet train her son, and as a special education teacher this was a great reward for him.

AAME#4 One positive moment he experienced was when he saw the impact of his influence on a student, and was able to relate with him. The parent was very pleased with him as a positive African American male teacher. She felt like her son had only been exposed to black males who were a bad influence and violent, and who liked to smoke, drink, and fight. The parent said it was very refreshing to have him in her son's life.

AAME# 5 One of the most memorable experiences is when one of the students he taught was killed based on his street involvement. One memorable parent experience was working with a parent as much as he could, but still, the parent stated that the school has failed the student. The parent was an enabler for the student.

AAME#6 The requests he gets from parents to get students to come in his class or simply spend time with him. The most memorable experience that he has had was a male student who was really attached to him and wanted him to teach him the following years. He didn't want to go to, and aside from the P.E. teacher, who was also an African American male teacher, he would have rather stayed with him.

AAME#7 His experience at a moving on ceremony was that a parent asked if he could say something. The parent thanked the staff, but also gave him a special thank you and the student still remains in contact. Also, one student asked him to help him study for the military.

AAME#8 He remembers when one student came into his 1st grade class not knowing his letters and sounds and by the time he left he was reading on a 4th grade level. One parent experience he had in his first year at his current school was when a parent accused him of bullying his child and came up to the school to confront him about it. After it was all said and done the parent realized the allegations were not true.

AAME#9 His most memorable moment was when a curious parent asked to come and observe his class because her child spoke about him all the time, however, he didn't take this request as a positive in the beginning. The parent came to several classes to observe him and was pleased to see how well the students responded to him. His student experience was working in the community he grew up in and seeing children he has worked with in the school approach him in the community and say "Hey, I love you" and then introduce him to their family.

AAME#10 He stated that his most memorable experience was doing a self-contained class with a student who didn't like math, but after working with him he began to love math and became good at it. He also remembers parent volunteers who came in three times a week and worked with the kids.

AAME# 11 The most memorable experience was when he ran into the parent of a former student and discovered the student had been killed. The parent revealed that out of all his teachers he was the only teacher he talked about. His greatest reward with students was watching his students who were told that they couldn't pass the SOL test actually pass the test.

11. Illustrate a time where you felt any bias or prejudice as an African American male in your school or school division.

AAME#1 Anytime he tries to make changes on anything based on the building administrator's vision it causes biases. Leaders are often hesitant to change and the decisions made are not always data driven.

AAME#2 Usually a desired commodity in the elementary school setting, there have been times when a female-dominated administration was or seemed to be in inequitable when assigning challenging students.

AAME#3 The only time he felt a bias was when he had a female superintendent and she didn't take the time to listen to what he had to say. He believes that more focus should be placed on the appropriate administrators who have experience working with teachers. You can have a great lesson plan but not know how to manage your classroom.

Back in the day you used to need to have more experience as an administrator as opposed to now, where with two years of experience you can be an administrator.

AAME#4 His bias is based on peoples' beliefs that the male is supposed to demand respect from all children at all times.

AAME# 5 Working in an area where the community was an affluent Caucasian-dominated population he experienced some obvious racial tensions.

AAME#6 The only bias he experienced was that he can be a savior to the male student who has extreme behavior issues.

AAME#7 Has never experienced any bias. Most people are happy he is around.

AAME#8 He doesn't feel like he is dealt an even hand because he is an African American male and is always getting more challenging students than the female teachers.

AAME#9 In the beginning he was expected to know how to do everything from working in the classroom to working on staff cars. He had to hide out at the close of the year because as the only male at the time he had to take boxes out to people's cars.

AAME#10 He has never felt any bias in his experience.

AAME#11 Once incentive pay was denied based on him moving from one building to the next. He was supposed to get his pay but he was denied by the female administrator at his former building. The end result was he went to higher administration, shared his concern, and received his money. He has only experience this bias from females.

12. Does the K-12 educational experience and life experience factor into African American males deciding to not enter the teaching profession? Why or why not?

AAME#1 Absolutely. Most males have not had a smooth transition in school. Some teachers take pride in failing male students, especially guys who look a certain way, perhaps hip-hop dressing students are looked at differently and judged more harshly as opposed to students who don't sag their pants or look a certain way. Often the bad teachers have had such a powerful influence over the students to the degree that students don't want to go into education. He never had a male content teacher during his high school career. He had a male shop teacher but never a male content teacher.

AAME#2 He believes that this was a major factor in his life because, after growing up in a predominately white educational system where there were very few opportunities to observe an intelligent African American male, he would have loved the opportunity to be taught by an African American male or someone who looked like him or shared the same culture.

AAME#3 The problem is many black males aren't going to school and some of them only focus on athletics as opposed to education. They mostly have a lot of pipe dreams of going to the NFL or NBA even though they have a better chance of becoming a teacher, doctor, or lawyer, and the parent is the greatest supporter.

AAME#4 He believes that it does. Sometimes after spending 12 years in school you may not want to go back into school to work and some adults just don't like dealing with children. He believes the people with the sharpest minds don't go into education because they can't handle the youth of today so they choose to go into other professions like engineering.

AAME#5 He believes that the K-12 experience does affect the reason as to why African American males don't go into the profession. Students have African American males as role models. Students have to see them in the profession to see that it works. Students have to see their quality of life is important and see the experience as a positive one.

AAME#6 A lot of teachers, female in particular, believe that males have behavior issues, but he believes that they are often misunderstood. He believes that their experience does make them dislike school and as a result they don't continue education in general or pursue it as a profession.

AAME#7 You rarely hear anyone tell a student that they would be a great teacher but you do hear people tell students that they will be great athletes. STEM for example, doesn't promote students entering education, but education promotes STEM. There is such a lack of encouragement to go into the profession.

AAME#8 He believes that the K-12 experience does affect the decision of African American males not to enter the teaching profession. He feels like if a student has a positive experience his decision may be different. The participant's personal experience allowed him to do peer tutoring as a student.

AAME#9 He believes that based on the high school experience not being a positive experience for many African American males, as a result they don't choose to go into the profession.

AAME#10 He believes that most males don't come into education, not because they don't like it, but because they don't believe they can make it through the whole day with kids. They simply need the experience.

AAME#11 The impact is so great because as an African American male he's providing real life experience for his students. He believes that African American males have a higher impact on students because he is a real life example of this.

13. **There have been wide ranging debates about the belief that African American male teachers have a positive impact on the academic performance of African American male students. What are your thoughts on this theory?**

AAME#1 If you take the time to build a relationship with the student, then yes, but without building a positive relationship with the student this may not be the case.

AAME#2 He wholeheartedly agrees based on his experiences and observations. He has observed relationships that Caucasian students have had with their Caucasian professors in predominantly white colleges or universities, and witnessed a strong connection between teacher and student, which ultimately increases student achievement. Consequently, when matriculating at an HBCU he experience the same opportunity to experience a culturally advantageous student-teacher relationship which undeniably instills confidence, connections, and an essential view of self-worth.

AAME#3 He believes that African American males have a greater impact on African American males students than anyone. He believes that students have to have a good role model that holds students to a higher level of expectation.

AAME#4 He believes that they do have a positive impact. He feels that if student trusts you then you can teach them. He feels like a student that has a Caucasian teacher may feel like they don't understand them so it's more challenging for a black student to trust them.

AAME#5 He saw an African American male teacher working in the profession motivating the students to excel to do their very best and he became a mentor.

AAME#6 Yes, he feels that the African American males in his class are really inspired to do the work because they see an African American male can do it. Often in low-income communities African American males don't have many positive roles models.

AAME#7 Yes, they would. The only teacher's name he remembers in school was an African American male.

AAME#8 The participant feels like an African American male has a greater impact than others on the African American male students. He believes that if the students see him being successful that they will gravitate to the profession.

AAME#9 He believes that him being an African American male is an asset to the students and that students can relate better to males as opposed to females. Normally kids respond and listen more to him as a male as opposed to a female teacher based on the ability to connect.

AAME#10 The participant believes that he has a greater impact on black students. He believes that the students need to see our goals in life, how we act in public, and how we act with groups of people. Interaction plays a major part.

AAME#11 The participant had several African American male teachers who taught him the importance of staying in school and how respect will take you a long way in life.

14. During your personal experience in school did you ever have an African American male teacher and what was their impact on your academic performance? If you did not have the opportunity to have an African American male teacher, what type of impact do you think it would have had on your school experience?

AAME#1 He has had two African American male teachers that were shop teachers. The teachers taught him that no matter what type of work you do, hard work pays off, and that you have to work hard at being the best at what you're doing. These two teachers had a positive impact on him and without this impact he could have developed a lazy mindset. The philosophy was whatever you start you must finish and not give up.

AAME#2 He personally experienced an 8th grade African American male teacher who instilled pride though high expectations and his ability to support him every step of the way.

AAME#3 He had a coach that took the time to try and mold him from being a gangster to being someone productive. He was inspired by him. No one in his family could even vote; he was the only one who can as a result of this experience. The person was the history teacher and coach.

AAME#4 He had one African American male teacher who was an electronics teacher. The participant doesn't really remember how or even if he impacted him academically.

AAME#5 His 6th grade teacher was ad African American male who had a huge impact on him. He served him in a dual capacity as teacher and coach. This is the person who instilled strong work ethics with in him and also motivation as a mentor playing basketball. The teacher took a real interest in him and held him to a high level of accountability.

AAME#6 Yes, he had an African American male teacher who inspired him to read more and pay close attention to issues that African Americans faced. That inspired him to become an educator.

AAME#7 His African American science teacher had a huge impact on him and he remembers the science project that he did and knows he uses science.

AAME#8 He had several African American male teachers; in fact he had five of them, but feels like he was self-motivated and his goal was to impact the teacher. He wanted to make his dead mother proud of him.

AAME#9 He only had one African American teacher and he was very instrumental. The teacher was his coach and P.E, teacher. He provided him with the opportunity to go to college by going above and beyond to support him and help him with getting into college.

AAME#10 The participant had two African American male teachers—one was a science teacher and one was a gym teacher. They impacted him because he watched the two of them as if they were under a microscope. Everything they said and did he took very seriously.

AAME#11 The participant had several African American male teachers who taught him the importance of staying in school and how respect will take you a long way in life.

15. Do you believe as an African American male that your school division has provided enough support for attracting and retaining African American male teachers? Please explain.

AAME#1 He says there is not enough support to attract or retain, and that it feels like a sink or swim world. The young African American males that he has worked with have not made it past three years and they are licensed teachers. Often the leaders of schools have been females and normally they have not provided the proper support needed, especially in this division. Administrators do not honor a referral coming from a male teacher and they often say it's a classroom management issue.

AAME#2 He said no, because in order to truly attract the number of African American males needed we have to illustrate a positive prospective of the African American teacher to students at an early age. The teaching profession has to be manifested in the eyes of the K-12 students in the same way that professional sports are for professional athletes.

AAME#3 He said yes, but thinks they need to turn them into administrators to provide more structure for the African American male.

AAME#4 From his experience he would say yes. He was a student-teacher and the principal called him in, interviewed him, and he got the job. He feels the division is actively seeking African American males.

AAME#5 He believes that the location that you're working in or living in plays a huge role in the hiring of African Americans.

AAME#6 He thinks they would like more but have a tough time finding African American male teachers.

AAME#7 The participant says no, because there is no real incentive to get them.

AAME#8 He said yes. He did his student-teaching in the division and due to having a newborn baby he had to make a decision to get a job immediately.

AAME# 9 He believes more needs to be done in this area.

AAME#10 The participant says yes, however, there is so much more to do.

AAME#11 He responded yes, but says the division has to provide more of what African American male teachers want.

16. Finally, what would be your advice for strengthening, recruiting, and retaining African American male teachers in elementary?

AAME#1 He believes there has to be something started on a larger scale to expose the impact African American male teachers can have on students. The universities/colleges need to bring more focus and positive attention to the impact that African American males have on education, so that their numbers in the education profession would increase. Exposure to the ins and outs of being an elementary educator is critical.

AAME#2 He says that literally, African American males that are strong, positive role models need to illuminate the profession and continue to encourage, nurture, and advocate for an increase in the success of African American males in education.

AAME#3 He believes that there has been a sizeable package for men to be able to take care of their family. With a wife and kid you have to have more money.

AAME#4 He believes that you have to attack the universities. As a member of the 3M Society, they went to other departments to convince them to come into education and were successful recruiting other students into the education major.

AAME# 5 He believes by attending college and recruitment fairs you can seek strong mentorships. It will help you to specialize in certain areas; for example, he was in speech pathology.

AAME#6 He believes there needs to be more funding, and also believes that there are African American males who do have the degrees needed but there needs to be more promotion of the profession to men at job fairs.

AAME#7 He believes if there was a bonus attached to the profession it would help, and also if schools provided seminars to encouraged men it would promote teachers coming into the school system. As students go through college they could have some conferences to promote the profession that are free or no cost. It has to be embedded into the minds of students to go into the profession.

AAME#8 He believes that more African American males in leadership and principal roles would motivate others to come into the profession. He believes that if the universities would have more male teachers go into the schools and promote the profession this would be a great way of recruiting them. Expressing the need to have them come into the profession would make a huge difference.

AAME#9 He believe that more colleges should forge working relationships with local universities, whether by providing funding or interview strategies to help support African Americans come into the profession. The local schools and colleges could collaboratively work together and promote careers in the education profession.

AAME#10 He believes we have to get them involved just to try it out. He says they need to see it and experience it on a personal basis.

AAME#11 He says there needs to be a forum to attract more African America men during the time they are in college. These men need to know what a positive impact they will have on students and how unfavorable it can be without them. There has to be a financial increase across the board to attract more males into the profession, because if the money is not worthy of the work men may not be attracted to leave the profession.

Summary on Motivating African American Males to Enter the Educational Profession

The purpose of this phenomenological study was to explore the perceptions and experiences of African American male K-5 elementary teachers as related to the underrepresentation of African American males in the teaching profession. The responses to the questions presented revealed the perceptions, thoughts, beliefs, and mindsets concerning the underrepresentation of African American males in the elementary education profession. The data analysis revealed 100 percent of the participants were in support of employing more African American males as teachers and achieving a racial balance to the teaching force in America.

The research states that the motivation to enter the elementary education profession would have to be intrinsic; African American males entering the K-5 elementary education profession would have to have a passion to serve students and cultivate children. The research shows that extrinsic factors do play a vital role in recruiting and retaining the individual in the profession. The extrinsic factors such as job security and benefits were indicators as the main motivators to help keep African American males in the teaching profession.

The participants revealed the shortage of African American males in education is a result of society and community issues. Based on their comments, more African American males are entering prison and jail than graduating from high school and college; hence, the shortage is a result of the lack of candidates. If a person does not possess the necessary education and experience, they cannot be recruited.

According to the study's participants, the African American community has also devalued education by choosing to glorify professions such as sports and entertainment. Education is often viewed as a secondary route to success. The African American community has to make education a top priority as a means to help produce more candidates who are eligible for the teaching profession.

The participants revealed African American male educators could have a positive impact on the academic performance of African American male students. Among the participants, some spoke of their own positive experiences of having an African American male teacher when they were in school, or the success of African American male students they have taught. The participants associated this success to cultural synchronization, familiarity, and being taught by a person of similar background. The participants also suggested this as an important consideration because in today's society most African American male students are in need of a strong African American male to be involved in their life and the teacher can fill a void.

The participants divulged that recruiting African American males into the teaching profession would be beneficial. The participants believed the two most viable recruitment tools would be financial incentives and exposure to the profession. Financial incentives could include, but not be limited to, higher salaries, bonuses, scholarships for postsecondary education, and loan repayment. The increased monetary incentives would attract highly qualified candidates who would strongly consider entering the teaching profession over the corporate world. Exposing potential teachers to the profession would draw candidates. Having high school students experience the teaching profession through job shadowing, internships, and apprenticeships would provide the students with an intimate view of the career. Students would be offered firsthand experience of the joys of teaching.

Four emerging themes were revealed through the course of the data analysis. The emerging themes were revealed as common phrases and statements consistently mentioned by the participants. The emerging themes can be used to create generalizations about the phenomena. The four emerging themes were (a) promotion of the profession, (b) monetary/financial incentives, (c) desire to help others, and (d) community support.

REFERENCES

Websites

- Learning Point Associates
  http://www.ncrel.org/sdrs/areas/issues/content/cntareas/math/ma8african.htm

This website is a valuable tool and resource that references after school programs, school improvement, literacy, math and science, teacher quality, technology, and NCREL data. The website is primarily directed at teachers and professionals

- Instructional Technology Center: College of Education-Georgia State University
  http://www.2gsu.edu/~dschjb/wwwmbti.html

This website provides a vast amount of resources for parents, educators, students, and professionals.

- HighBeam Encyclopedia, http://encyclopedia.com/doc/1G1-62839470.html

This website contains a vast amount of information relating to news articles, student journals, and academic journals. The website is a productive resource for parents, teachers, and professionals.

- *Differences Between African American and Caucasian Students on Critical Thinking and Learning Style*, Gadzella, Bernadette M., Huang, Jiafen, Masten, William G. Study of African American and Caucasian students determining critical thinking can be defined. The resource is beneficial to teachers and professionals in education.
- *Learning Styles of African American Children*, Carrie L. Francis. The learning style differences stem from the way African Americans learn and express information. The document is useful for students, parents, teachers, and professionals.

DEFINITIONS/TERMS

Academic performance is the level of performance a student displays in an educational setting including grade point average, standardized test scores, and honors received (Bonneville Power Administration, 2004).

Achievement gap is the disparity in academic performance between groups of students most often used to describe performance gaps. The achievement gap shows up in grades, standardized-test scores, course selection, dropout rates, and college-completion rates. It has become a focal point of education reform efforts (Williams, 2012).

African-American is a person of black African decent born in the United States of America (Merriam-Webster, 2010).

Caucasian is a person of European origin often referred to as white (Farlex, 2010).

Cultural relevancy empowers students intellectually, socially, emotionally, and politically by using cultural referents to impart knowledge, skills, and attitudes (Ladson-Billings, 1995).

Disadvantaged student are students whose families are eligible to participate in the federal free and reduced price lunch program (U.S. Department of Health and Human Services, 2004).

No Child Left Behind is the Elementary and Secondary Education Act of 1965, which created the Title I federal aid program aimed at reducing achievement gaps between high social economic statues students and low social economic statues students (National Education Association, 2002). NCLB ties federal dollars for any school, which cannot meet a series of one-size-fits-all standards. 7

Pseudonym is a name that a person or group assumes for a particular purpose, which differs from his or her original or true name (Merriam-Webster, 2010).

Role model is a person whose success can be emulated by others, especially younger people (Dictionary, 2010).

Teacher-student cultural synchronization is the connection a teacher and student share through similar backgrounds, cultural identities, and commonalities used to build and foster relationships (Irvine, 2002).

Printed in the United States
By Bookmasters